Conten

£1

88

Knitting Patterns

98

Craft Makes

38

Recipes

JANUARY

29 Dec 2014

30 Dec 2014

31 Dec 2014

1 Thursday BANK HOLIDAY

2 Friday

3 Saturday

4 Sunday

COVER UP
Your Cushions

Use textured stitches and berry shades to add a cosy and inviting touch to your sofa cushions

- ✸ Easy-peasy
- ✸ **A Bit More Tricky**
- ✸ Hard-ish
- ✸ Quite A Challenge

BOBBLE AND RIB CUSHION

MEASUREMENTS
46 x 46cm/18 x 18in.

MATERIALS
6 x 50g balls of Sirdar Big Softie Super Chunky (51% wool, 49% acrylic) in Fripp (324). Pair of 9mm (No. 00) knitting needles. 45cm square cushion pad; 4 buttons.
You can buy the yarn online at womansweeklyshop.com/yarn or call 0800 024 1212.

TENSION
9 stitches and 12 rows, to 10 x 10cm, over pattern, using 9mm needles.

ABBREVIATIONS
K, knit; **p**, purl; **st**, stitch; **tog**, together; **mb**, make bobble (work k1, p1, k1, p1 all in next st, turn, p4, turn, k4, turn, p2tog, p2tog, turn, k2tog); **yrn**, yarn round needle to make a st.

NOTE
Yarn amounts are based on average requirements and are therefore approximate. Instructions in square brackets are worked as stated after 2nd bracket.

TO MAKE
Lower back: With 9mm needles, cast on 42 sts.
1st row: K5, [p5, k4] to last 10 sts, p5, k5. **2nd row:** P5, [k5, p4] to last 10 sts, k5, p5.
Repeat last 2 rows, 16 times more. Mark each end of last row for fold edge.
Front: 1st row: K5, [p5, k4] to last 10 sts, p5, k5. **2nd row:** P5, [k5, p4] to last 10 sts, k5, p5. **3rd and 4th rows:** As 1st and 2nd rows.
5th row: K5, [p2, mb, p2, k4] to last 10 sts, p2, mb, p2, k5. **6th row:** As 2nd row. **7th to 12th rows:** Repeat 1st and 2nd rows, 3 times.
Repeat last 12 rows, 3 times more, then work 1st to 8th rows again. Mark each end of last row for fold edge.

Upper back: 1st row: K5, [p5, k4] to last 10 sts, p5, k5. **2nd row:** P5, [k5, p4] to last 10 sts, k5, p5.
Repeat last 2 rows, 13 times more.
Buttonhole row: Rib 7, [yrn, p2tog, rib 7] 3 times, yrn, p2tog, rib 6.
Rib another 5 rows. Cast off in rib. Fold back pieces at markers lapping upper back over lower back by 12 rows and secure lapped-over edges on outside. Join side seams. Sew on buttons. Insert pad and button up to close.

LEAF CUSHION

MEASUREMENTS
46 x 46cm/18 x 18in.

MATERIALS
1 x 400g ball of Hayfield Bonus Aran (80% acrylic, 20% wool) in Purple Heather (871); 1 ball of Sirdar Country Style DK (40% nylon, 30% wool, 30% acrylic) in each of Silver Cloud (434), Pansy (471) and Rosehip (527). Pair of 3¾mm (No. 9) and 4½mm (No. 7) knitting needles. A 45cm square cushion pad; 30cm-long zip fastener.
You can buy the yarn online at womansweeklyshop.com/yarn or call 0800 024 1212.

TENSION
19 stitches and 25 rows, to 10 x 10cm, over stocking stitch, using Aran yarn and 4½mm needles.

ABBREVIATIONS
K, knit; **p,** purl; **st,** stitch; **ss,** stocking stitch (k on right side and p on wrong side); **s2kpo,** slip next 2 sts as if about to work them together, k1, then pass 2 slip st over.

NOTE
Yarn amounts are based on average requirements and are therefore approximate.

FRONT AND BACK
(both alike)
With 4½mm needles and Purple Heather, cast on 88 sts.
Ss 114 rows. Cast off.

SMALL LEAF
With 3¾mm needles and Feather Grey, cast on 9 sts.
1st row: P4, k1, p4. **2nd row:** K4, p1, k4. **3rd row:** K twice in first st, k2, s2kpo, k1, k twice in next st, k1.
4th row: P. **5th to 8th rows:** As 1st to 4th rows. **9th and 10th rows:** As 1st and 2nd rows.

11th row: K3, s2kpo, k3 – 7 sts.
12th row: P. **13th row:** P2, s2kpo, p2 – 5 sts. **14th row:** K2, p1, k2.
15th row: K1, s2kpo, k1 – 3 sts.
16th row: P. **17th row:** S2kpo.
Fasten off.
Make 5 more small leaves in Feather Grey and 6 in each of Pansy and Damson.

LARGE LEAF
With 3¾mm needles and Feather Grey, cast on 13 sts.
1st row: P6, k1, p6. **2nd row:** K6, p1, k6. **3rd row:** K twice in first st, k4, s2kpo, k3, k twice in next st, k1.
4th row: P. **5th to 8th rows:** As 1st to 4th rows. **9th and 10th rows:** As 1st and 2nd rows.

11th row: K5, s2kpo, k5 – 11 sts.
12th row: P. **13th row:** P5, k1, p5.
14th row: K5, p1, k5.
15th row: K4, s2kpo, k4 – 9 sts.
16th row: P. **17th row:** P4, k1, p4.
18th row: K4, p1, k4.
19th row: K3, s2kpo, k3 – 7 sts.
20th row: P. **21st row:** P2, s2kpo, p2 – 5 sts. **22nd row:** K2, p1, k2.
23rd row: K1, s2kpo, k1 – 3 sts.
24th row: P.
25th row: S2kpo. Fasten off.
Make 1 more large leaf in Feather Grey and 2 in each of Pansy and Damson.

TO MAKE UP
Arrange leaves on front of cushion as in photo. Sew leaves to cushion with a line of chain stitches work along centre ridge, then continue for couple more stitches below each leaf for stalk.
Join back and front together around all sides, leaving a 30cm opening on one side. Sew in zip to open edge. Insert pad and close zip.

BASKET-WEAVE CUSHION

MEASUREMENTS
46 x 46cm/18 x 18in.

MATERIALS
4 x 50g balls of Sirdar Softspun Chunky (53% nylon, 24% wool, 23% acrylic) in Shale (581). Pair of 5mm (No. 6) knitting needles. A 45cm square cushion pad; 8 buttons.
For yarn stockists, call Sirdar

Spinning Ltd on 01924 371501, or visit sirdar.co.uk

TENSION
16 stitches and 25 rows, to 10 x 10cm, over pattern, using 5mm needles.

ABBREVIATIONS
K, knit; **p,** purl; **st,** stitch; **tog,** together; **yf,** yarn forward to make a st.

NOTE
Yarn amounts are based on average requirements and are therefore approximate. Instructions in square brackets are worked as stated after 2nd bracket.

TO MAKE
Left front: With 5mm needles, cast on 75 sts.
1st row: P5, [k5, p5] to end.
2nd row: K5, [p5, k5] to end.
3rd row: As 1st row. **4th row:** P.
5th row: K5, [p5, k5] to end.
6th row: P5, [k5, p5] to end.
7th row: As 5th row. **8th row:** P.
These 8 rows form pattern.
Pattern another 56 rows.
Mark each end of last row for fold edge.
Back: Pattern another 115 rows. Mark each end of last row for fold edge.
Right front: Pattern another 57 rows.
Buttonhole row: Pattern 2, [yf, k2tog, pattern 8] 7 times, yf, k2tog, pattern 1.
Pattern another 6 rows.
Cast off in pattern.
Fold fronts at markers lapping right front over left front by 12 rows, and secure lapped-over edges on outside. Join top and lower edge seams. Sew on buttons. Insert pad and button up to close.

POST – CARD

Reader Margaret Posselt, from Polokwane in South Africa, nominates the Victoria Falls in Africa

'My favourite place is most definitely the Victoria Falls on the border of Zambia and Zimbabwe. Paradoxically, in spite of the thundering waterfall, it really is a remarkably peaceful place, and it's marvellous to watch the baboons coming to drink in the pools. I could live there forever!'

5 Monday

6 Tuesday

7 Wednesday

8 Thursday

9 Friday

10 Saturday

11 Sunday

Minted Lamb Cobbler

Serves 3-4
Calories: 822
Fat: 40g
Saturated fat: 15g
Suitable for freezing: ✔

* 3 tablespoons olive oil
* 6 rasher smoked streaky bacon, chopped
* 250g (8oz) shallots, peeled
* 350g (12oz) Chantenay carrots or baby carrots
* 2 parsnips, peeled and chopped
* 400-500g packet diced lamb
* 2 tablespoons plain flour
* 300ml (½ pint) red wine
* 1 lamb stock cube
* 1 tablespoon chopped fresh mint
* 1 teaspoon Marmite
* Salt and freshly ground black pepper

FOR THE TOPPING:
* 250g (8oz) self-raising flour
* 50g (1¾oz) butter
* 2 level tablespoons chopped fresh mint
* 1 medium egg
* Approx. 100ml (3½fl oz) milk

* 1.75 litre (3 pint) casserole dish
* 6.5cm (2¾in) plain round cutter

1 Set the oven to 180°C or Gas Mark 4. Heat 1 tablespoon oil in a sauté pan and add the bacon and shallots. Cook over a medium heat for 5-7 minutes, until they start to brown. Add the carrots and parsnips to the pan, and cook for a further 3-4 minutes. Tip the contents of the pan into the casserole dish.

2 Return the pan to the heat and add the remaining oil. When the oil is very hot, add the meat to the pan. Cook the meat over a high heat for 4-5 minutes, turning it occasionally to brown the outside, but taking care not to turn it too much, as the meat will brown better if left to sear on each surface. Sprinkle the flour over the meat and stir to coat it. Pour in the red wine, and stir well and bring to the boil and simmer for a few minutes. Pour in 300ml (½ pint) water and crumble in the stock cube. Add the mint, Marmite and seasoning. Pour the mixture into the casserole. Cover the dish, either with a lid or foil, and cook in the centre of the oven for 1½-1¾ hours.

3 To make the scones for the topping, tip the flour into a bowl and rub in the butter. Stir in the mint and season. Beat the egg with enough milk to make it up to 150ml (¼ pint). Reserve about 2 tablespoons egg mixture and pour the rest into the flour. Use a round-bladed knife to mix the ingredients into a dough. Turn the dough out on to the work surface and knead it very lightly to give a smooth surface.

4 Roll the dough out on a floured surface and cut out about 8 rounds, about 2.5cm (1in) thick, re-rolling the trimmings as necessary.

5 Working quickly, take the casserole out of the oven. Place the scones on top and brush with reserved egg mixture, then return the dish to the oven, uncovered, for 20-30 minutes, or until the scones have risen. Serve immediately with mashed potatoes and steamed green vegetables.

❋ **To freeze:** The scone topping is not suitable for freezing. The stew can be packed into a freezer container when cold and frozen for up to 1 month. Let it defrost before reheating and cooking with the scones.

Tip from our kitchen
If you don't like Marmite, leave it out and add a good dash of Worcestershire sauce.

Your Good Health

Ask Dr Mel

Q My husband has depression and it's hard to help him. Now it's really getting me down, too. Where can I find support?

A It's incredibly hard when someone we love is depressed. Plus, if we have never been depressed ourselves, their low mood, lack of enthusiasm, negative thinking, withdrawal and irritability can be extremely difficult to understand. And although we try our best to be sympathetic and offer practical suggestions, we may run out of ideas (or patience) if these seem to make no difference. We may also be missing the emotional and practical support that person normally gives us, struggle to keep all the balls in the air, and wonder if they'll ever get back to their normal selves. We often end up feeling guilty, or are too embarrassed and/or loyal to discuss this with other people.

But you do need to look after yourself as well. Do you have any trusted family members or friends that you could talk things over with, confidentially? You could also discuss your own feelings with your doctor, or benefit from counselling or even medication yourself.

You may find a new book, *Severe Depression – The Essential Guide For Carers* by Tony Frais, or the Royal College of Psychiatrists' information (020 7235 2351; rcpsych.ac.uk) helpful, too.

TAKE 5...
Ways To Protect Your Heart

1 EAT MORE fresh fibre from fruit and vegetables, and less salt and fat.

2 TAKE 30 minutes' exercise, five times a week.

3 MAINTAIN a healthy weight and a BMI below 25 (that's your weight in kilograms divided by your height in metres multiplied by itself).

4 GET your blood pressure and cholesterol levels checked at least once every five years.

5 DRINK alcohol only in moderation and don't smoke.

A Great Exercise To...
Strengthen your thighs

Forward Lunge

Stand with feet hip-width apart, then take a big step forward with your left leg, and lower your body towards the floor. Your back knee should point to the floor, front knee in line with your ankle (not over your foot). Return to the starting position. Repeat by stepping forward with your right leg. To increase the effort, hold a full bottle of water in each hand. Repeat 10 times on each side. *Well done!*

TIP
Now try a reverse lunge (step back rather than forward). You may wobble to start with, but your balance will improve after a few goes.

HOW THE EXPERTS STAY HEALTHY
Neil Shah, stress-management expert

What's in your medicine cabinet?
Echinacea, to boost my immune system and make me more resilient; and aloe-vera gel, for cuts and sunburn.

What's good in your fridge?
Lots of green vegetables – watercress, spinach, rocket, kale – for salads and green smoothies.

What's your favourite exercise?
I'm passionate about running. I'm currently training for my fifth marathon. It allows me to be at one with nature, a form of moving meditation. I also love playing football: team sports are a wonderful way to catch up with friends and a great stress reliever.

What's a special treat?
It's usually fresh strawberries with frozen vanilla yogurt – lovely!

Do you have any good tips for coping with stress?
Build the relaxation muscle. You don't go to the gym once and expect to be fit for life. In the same way, we have to relax regularly if we're to build our ability to deal with stress.

What's a childhood remedy that still works for you?
Honey, ginger and lemon to beat a chill or to help with a cold or a sore throat.

● *The 10-Step Stress Solution* by Neil Shah (Ebury, £9.99) is out now. For more information, visit stress.org.uk

12 Monday

13 Tuesday

14 Wednesday

15 Thursday

16 Friday

17 Saturday

18 Sunday

Cosy Canine

Use your favourite fabrics to sew this colourful pet bed for a four-legged family member – it's washable, too!

Finished size: 70 x 15cm

YOU WILL NEED
- A2 sheet of paper or greaseproof paper
- HB pencil and ruler
- 140cm of 112cm-wide lightweight white cotton fabric
- 240cm of 112cm-wide patterned cotton fabric

MAIN INSTRUCTIONS GIVEN ARE FOR A SMALL DOG
- 70cm of 90cm-wide natural calico fabric
- 51cm zip
- 700g washable toy filling
- Drawing pin
- String
- Matching sewing threads

Lovely Folk Heart Grey fabric (pictured), from a selection at Fabric Rehab (fabricrehab.co.uk)

And if your dog needs a bit more leg room...

FOR A MEDIUM-SIZED DOG
Finished size: 80 x 15cm
YOU WILL NEED
- 150cm of 112cm-wide lightweight white cotton fabric
- 240cm of 112cm-wide patterned cotton fabric
- 80cm of 90cm-wide natural calico fabric
- 56cm zip
- 900g washable toy filling

Template: Draw a 72cm semicircle.
Cutting out: Cut two 112 x 39cm rectangles for the rim.
Step 1 – leave a 56cm gap in seam for zip.

FOR A LARGE DOG
Finished size: 90 x 15cm
YOU WILL NEED
- 170cm of 112cm-wide lightweight white cotton fabric
- 3m of 112cm-wide patterned cotton fabric
- 90cm of 90cm-wide natural calico fabric
- 56cm zip
- 1 kilo washable toy filling

Template: Draw an 82cm semicircle.
Cutting out: Cut three 86 x 39cm rectangles for the rim.
Step 1 – leave a 56cm gap in seam for zip.

MAKING THE TEMPLATE

Using the pencil and ruler, draw a horizontal line 62cm long and a vertical line 31cm long on a sheet of paper, as shown on the diagram *(opposite)*, then mark the middle of the horizontal line, labelling it 'Place to fold'. Draw another 62cm horizontal line 1.5cm down from the 'Place to fold' line and label 'Back cutting line'. Fix a drawing pin through the centre mark. Tie a pencil to length of string, hold the pencil upright on one end of the line and tie the end of the string to the drawing pin, keeping the string taut, so it is 31cm long. Draw a semicircle between the ends of back cutting line. Cut out the template.

CUTTING OUT

1 For the cushion cover and rims: Using the patterned fabric, cut one pair of 95.5 x 39cm rectangles for the bed rim, cutting the short edges parallel with the fabric selvedges. Then cut one pair of semicircles, cutting along the back cutting line and one semicircle placed to the fold to open out to make a circle.

2 For the cushion pad liner: Using the lightweight white fabric, cut one pair of semicircles, cutting along the back cutting line, and one semicircle placed to the fold to open out to make a circle.

3 For the bed base: Using the calico, cut one semicircle to the fold to make a circle.

MAKING THE CUSHION PAD

1 Pin the two white semicircles together, right sides facing, then stitch the straight edges, taking a 1.5cm seam allowance and leaving a 20cm gap in the centre. Press the seam open. Pin the two circles together with right sides facing. Stitch the outer edges, taking a 1cm seam allowance. Clip the curves and press the seam open.

2 Turn the cushion pad right side out and stuff it evenly with toy filling. Slip stitch the gap closed.

MAKING THE CUSHION COVER

1 Pin the two patterned semicircles together, right sides facing, and stitch along the straight edges, taking a 1.5cm seam

allowance and leaving a 51cm opening in the centre. Next, tack the pinned opening edges together. Press the seam open. Lay the zip centrally along the seam, face down. Pin and tack the zip in place.

2 On the right side, use a zipper foot on the sewing machine to stitch the zip 6mm from the tacked seam and across the ends of the zip. Unpick the tacking and open the zip.

3 Pin the two circles together, with right sides facing. Stitch the outer edges, taking a 1cm seam allowance. Clip the curves and press the seam open. Turn the cushion right side out and insert the cushion pad. Close the zip.

MAKING THE BED BASE

1 Pin the two patterned rectangles, right sides facing, taking a 1cm seam allowance to make the rim. Pin and stitch the rims together along the short edges to form a ring, leaving a 12cm gap 2.5cm down from the top of one of the long edges in one seam. Press the seams open. Fold the rim lengthways in half with wrong sides facing and matching the seams. Pin the raw edges together.

2 Divide the raw edge of the rim and base into quarters and mark with a pin at each division. With right sides facing, pin the rim to the calico base, matching the pins and raw edges. Stitch all around the base, taking a 1cm seam allowance. Neaten the seam with a zigzag stitch or with pinking shears. Turn the seam to the inside of the bed. Place the cushion on the base. Stuff the rim evenly then slip stitch the gap securely closed with small stitches, using a double length of thread.

YOUR PATTERN TEMPLATE

31cm

1.5cm

PLACE TO FOLD

BACK CUTTING LINE (62cm)

Dad's Dream Job

Computer to fix? I'm your man. Running a home? That's a different matter...

It made sense for me to become a househusband when Ginny was headhunted by an international marketing firm. We both knew there was no way my salary would ever climb to the dizzy heights she was being offered. Besides, it was her dream job.

I was fed up too with all the office politics I was having to put up with.

If she took the job I could go freelance and work from home, schedule my days around Jamie's needs, giving him a constant parent in his life rather than changing child-minders. So, four months ago I officially became a freelance IT trouble-shooter and Ginny took another step up the high-flyer's ladder.

Have to admit it's been tougher than I'd anticipated. Give me a computer to fix, a gaming programme to write and I'm your man. Running a home efficiently was something I had to learn – and learn quickly.

Of course I'd been a hands-on dad with Jamie from the word go, but Ginny had always been around to do the basic household organising. It was a steep learning curve, that's for sure. Getting the order and the timing right for putting a meal on the table, sorting the washing, shopping, taking Jamie into his reception class at school and then remembering to collect him a few hours later, organising bath time, getting him to go to bed before collapsing with a cold beer on the sofa.

Then there was the routine housework – which, if I'm honest, in the beginning was just a quick flip around with the vacuum, beds pulled up and the dishwasher filled half an hour before Ginny arrived home each evening. Very little freelancing got done in those first few weeks, but we definitely had fun, Jamie and me.

One of the perks of being a househusband I revelled in for those first weeks was the freedom from clock-watching. Who cared if I had a nap during Jeremy Vine? Who cared if I ate lunch at twelve o'clock or two o'clock? Who cared if I switched the computer on the minute the school run was over, then proceeded to ignore it for the next three hours?

But gradually sense returned and a routine of sorts developed. Jamie and I began to eat less cereals for dinner and more vegetables. Clean school clothes started to reappear in the airing cupboard – un-ironed but clean. I even managed to fit some work in when Jamie's school hours were increased after his fifth birthday.

The mums at the school gate scared me ridged in the beginning. Hadn't realised there were so many career woman like Ginny around. I don't think there's more than two stay-at-home mums at the school gate and definitely no dads doing the regular run. If there are I haven't bumped into them yet.

The mothers I see every morning (au pairs and nannies seem to do the afternoon run) are real yummy mummies to the core – all high heels and business suits and designer briefcases presumably stuffed full of important papers, ready for the dash to the office.

Who cared if I had a nap during Jeremy Vine?

'Ginny is so lucky to have you, Ben,' one said to me yesterday morning as we each waved our respective child into school. 'Giving up your career for her.'

I smiled at her and shrugged. 'Not given up – just put it on hold for a bit. I'm doing freelance computing stuff from home.'

Silently I'd added, 'for the moment', remembering what was waiting for me on my computer.

An offer from my old company had pinged into my email box. It was hard to take in at first, but then I realised I was being offered my dream job by my old company. They wanted me to ring them to arrange an urgent meeting. I'd resisted the urge to phone immediately and make an appointment. I had to talk it over with Ginny first, but thinking about the offer made me want to punch the air.

Working at home is great and I love spending so much time with Jamie, but I do miss the office banter. No one to spar words with. No one to bounce ideas off. Accepting the job would give me that in spades. We'd have to get a childminder for Jamie. But would being met by a childminder at the end of the school day be that bad? A day or two – maybe a week – of disruption while he got used to it, and then another routine would be established and become the norm in his life.

Ginny said the decision was mine. 'After all, I've got my dream job – why shouldn't you have one, too?'

Why not indeed? So why do I keep putting off the moment of ringing the office and making that life-changing appointment? I need to be really sure it's what I want and for some strange reason I don't feel one hundred per cent committed to accepting the offer.

When I picked Jamie up from school this afternoon we walked home slowly through the park. Autumn leaves were falling and Jamie laughed at the crunchy sound they made as he jumped on them.

'Miss has made a pumpkin light. Can we make one too?' he asked.

'Sure – and I'll make pumpkin soup with all the left over bits,' I said.

'I don't have to eat the soup if I don't like it, do I?' Jamie asked anxiously.

'No – just so long as you try it.'

'OK,' and he was off again, racing towards the playground.

Sitting on the bench watching him swing higher and higher, I smiled. Suddenly I realised we were both living utterly in the present. I wasn't sneakily checking my phone for texts, thinking about a meeting or trying to compose an email in my head.

I was enjoying time with my son in the park – and it felt so right. Dream job? Think I've already got it for the next few years.

THE END

© Jennifer Bohnet, 2013

19 Monday

20 Tuesday

21 Wednesday

22 Thursday

23 Friday

24 Saturday

25 Sunday

Wordsearch 1

Find all the listed birds in the grid except one – they run either forwards or backwards, horizontally, vertically or diagonally, but always in a straight unbroken line.
The missing word is your answer.

BLACKBIRD
BULLFINCH
CHAFFINCH
CUCKOO
CURLEW
GOLDFINCH
KITE
MAGPIE

MOORHEN
PARTRIDGE
PHEASANT
ROBIN
ROOK
SKYLARK
STARLING
SWIFT

B	B	U	L	L	F	I	N	C	H
L	H	C	U	R	L	E	W	C	G
A	E	C	O	S	H	T	N	T	N
C	C	O	N	R	E	I	E	N	I
K	K	U	O	I	F	K	I	A	L
B	S	O	C	D	F	B	P	S	R
I	M	W	L	K	O	F	G	A	A
R	X	O	I	R	O	X	A	E	T
D	G	E	S	F	T	O	M	H	S
E	G	D	I	R	T	R	A	P	C

Codeword

A codeword is like a crossword puzzle but there are no clues!

Every letter of the alphabet has been replaced by a number, the same number representing the same letter throughout the puzzle. Just decide which letter is represented by which number! To start you off, we reveal the codes for three letters. When you've filled in these letters throughout the puzzle, you'll have enough information to guess words and discover other letters. Use the letter checklist and letter grid to keep track of the letters you have found.

You can work it out...

A B C D E F G H I/J K L M N O P/Q R S/T U V W X Y Z

1	2	3	4 I	5	6	7	8	9	10	11	12	13
14	15	16	17	18	19	20	21	22	23	24 P	25	26 S

Solutions to this month's puzzle on March puzzles

SOLUTIONS FOR DECEMBER 2015

ACROSS 1 Athens **5** Escort **8** Flambeau **9** Rump **10** Opus **11** Imposing **12** Cohere **13** Assist **15** Together **18** Acer **19** Aeon **20** Ordnance **21** Assets **22** Ever so
DOWN 2 Telephoto lens **3** En masse **4** Sterile **5** Equip **6** Cards **7** Reminiscences **13** Abridge **14** Swanage **16** Ernie **17** Hooks

Answer: MOUSE

26 Monday

27 Tuesday

28 Wednesday

29 Thursday

30 Friday

31 Saturday

1 Sunday

FEBRUARY

2 Monday

_____

3 Tuesday

_____

4 Wednesday

_____

5 Thursday

_____

6 Friday

_____

7 Saturday

_____

8 Sunday

_____

Lucky Charm Bracelet

With its striking silver and blue theme, our easy-make bracelet is truly charming!

MAKING A LOOP

When you thread beads onto a head pin or want to attach something to a head pin, you need to form a loop. This will then, if needed, allow you to attach it to a necklace, chain or ear wire.

1 When attaching a bead, thread the bead onto the head pin, then cut off the excess wire about 1cm above the bead. Holding the wire vertically in your hand, use your round-nose pliers to bend it back at a right angle.

2 Holding the cut end of the wire tightly in your round-nose pliers, carefully curl the wire back to form a loop, following the contours of the pliers. Depending on the function of the loop you may either close it immediately or keep it slightly open so that you can attach something to it before closing.

OPENING AND CLOSING A JUMP RING

Don't open a jump ring by pulling the ends outwards as this will weaken it and you won't be able to return it to its original shape. Always use two pairs of pliers. We have used combination (snipe-nose) pliers and round-nose pliers.

1 To open a jump ring, grasp it on both sides with the pliers. Open the jump ring laterally, moving one end towards you and the other end away from you.

2 To close a jump ring, gently press the ends together as you bring them past one another. Bring them back together gently, compressing them as you do it.

When they come together a second time you should hear and feel a click – this tells you that the ring is closed with tension and will remain closed. If you don't hear the click, pass the ends by one another again until you hear the click.

Following our easy step-by-step instructions and how-to tips, you can make this trendy trinket bracelet, perfect for a gift or simply for you!

For this project you'll combine the 'Making a loop' technique with 'Opening and closing a jump ring'. The design can easily be adapted with your own chosen beads and charms.

You will need

- ❀ Round-nose pliers
- ❀ Combination pliers
- ❀ Wire cutters
- ❀ Ruler
- ❀ Silver-plated trace chain in medium weight 16cm length (for an average wrist), from a selection at The Bead and Jewellery Shop (020 8891 4920)
- ❀ Silver-plated T-bar clasp, from 45p, The Bead and Jewellery Shop (as before)
- ❀ Four 11mm oval blue beads, 8p each, The Bead and Jewellery Shop (as before)
- ❀ Five round 7mm blue opaque glass beads, The Bead and Jewellery Shop (as before)
- ❀ Seventeen 5mm silver-plated jump rings
- ❀ Nine x 1½in silver-plated head pins
- ❀ Nine x 5mm silver-plated plain bead caps
- ❀ Six charms (10mm sixpence, 8mm x 9mm thimble, 10mm x 10mm bell, 10mm button, 13mm x 8mm wishbone and 11mm x 12mm horseshoe), from a selection at Vivi Celebrations (020 8133 7123; vivicelebrations.com)

1 Cut the chain to length using the wire cutters. Open up a jump ring with pliers (see 'Opening and closing a jump ring' opposite far left).

2 Take the open jump ring and loop it through one end of the chain and through the 'T' part of the T-bar clasp to link them together. Close the jump ring up (see 'Opening and closing a jump ring' opposite left). Repeat to attach the other end of the chain to the circular end of the clasp with a jump ring.

3 Thread a bead cap onto a head pin and then a large blue bead. Trim the head pin above the bead allowing for about 1cm, to make a

loop. Make a closed loop using the round-nose pliers (see 'Making a loop' opposite left). Repeat with all the remaining small and large beads until all are wired up with loops.

4 Take the time to lay the beads and charms out in the order that you want and then evenly space them out along the chain. Alternate the beads and charms as much as you can. Once you are happy with the design, open up jump rings and attach one to each individual charm and bead, leaving them open.

5 Attach each bead and charm to the chain in the desired place, closing each jump ring up as you go to complete.

❀ **HOW-TO TIP** Always use two sets of pliers when opening and closing a jump ring. We have used round-nose pliers and combination pliers.

❀ **BEAD CAPS** are generally used with headpins to provide a covering for the top or bottom of a bead, and they add a nice finishing touch.

All Hands On Deck

Women of this age were adept with their hands. Whether creating something pretty or solving a need, where there was a will there was a way

THE FIRST PART OF OUR GIFT TO YOU.
The Pattern of these easily made Cooking Sleeves will be given with the envelope on Wednesday, Jan. 3rd.

Something for everyone
Smaller projects and simple patterns allowed women of all abilities to try their hands

Women's war effort
Sending 'Tommy' parcels of clothes was a small but important act of kindness

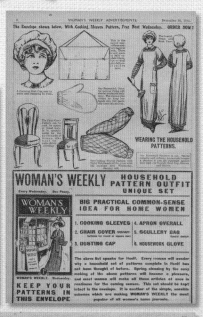

WEARING THE HOUSEHOLD PATTERNS.

A SCENTED DRESS-HANGER.
THE covering is made of a straight strip of ribbon, about three inches wide, and half as long again as the width of the hanger. To make the cover, mark the centre of the ribbon, and here cut and work a little eyelet to slip the hook through. Fold the ribbon lengthwise, to bring the bordered sides together, slip the hook through the eyelet, and run the bordered sides together just within the edges, so that the casing fits the hanger tightly. Draw the running thread up to make the fulness, and fasten off; then neaten the ends.

The hook is beautified by winding a strip of very narrow ribbon round and round it until it is covered. A few stitches here and there keep the ribbon in place.

The scent-bag is just made of a round of silk, hemmed at the edges, then gathered up tightly just over the filling of lavender.

Man's work
There were even ideas for husbands to try

This scheme for a rather basic 'rustic table for the garden' is somewhat light on instructions. While the basic premise is simple, the magazine's confidence that any amateur carpenter could recreate it easily demonstrates the expected standards of craftsmanship in early 20th-century homes. And, of course, it would have to be done without the aid of electronic power tools.

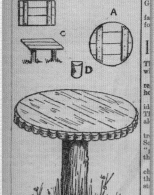

HOBBIES FOR HUBBIES.
What the Amateur Carpenter Can Do.
A Rustic Table.
A RUSTIC table for the garden can be made in almost any size to suit requirements.

The top is circular in shape, and is composed of four pieces of wood fastened together with bars of wood screwed on underneath, and Diagram A illustrates this and shows the underside of the table.

The edge is finished off with tiny pieces of split boughs of the shape shown in Diagram D, and these little pieces of wood are nailed in their places side by side.

The table is supported underneath with a tree-stump, and to hold it securely in its place long nails are driven through the centre of the surface and into the upper part of the stump.

This table can be made on exactly the same lines, but in a square shape, if preferred, and the wood for the surface fastened together in the same manner (Diagram B); but it will require two supports underneath, as shown in Diagram C.

9 Monday

10 Tuesday

11 Wednesday

12 Thursday

13 Friday

14 Saturday

15 Sunday

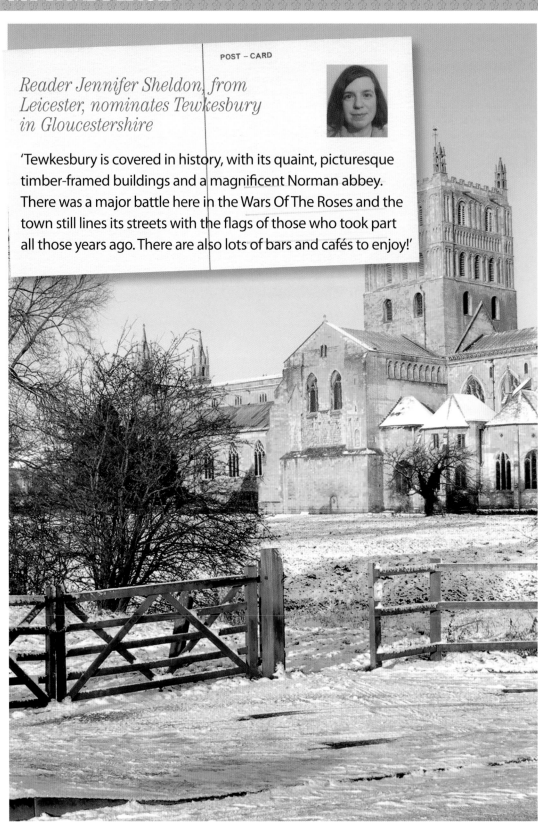

POST – CARD

Reader Jennifer Sheldon, from Leicester, nominates Tewkesbury in Gloucestershire

'Tewkesbury is covered in history, with its quaint, picturesque timber-framed buildings and a magnificent Norman abbey. There was a major battle here in the Wars Of The Roses and the town still lines its streets with the flags of those who took part all those years ago. There are also lots of bars and cafés to enjoy!'

16 Monday

17 Tuesday

18 Wednesday

19 Thursday

20 Friday

21 Saturday

22 Sunday

Triple Chocolate Cake

Serves 12-15
Calories: 625
Fat: 40g
Saturated fat: 23g
Suitable for freezing: ✔

FOR THE CAKE:
* 350g (12oz) butter, softened
* 350g (12oz) self-raising flour
* 350g (12oz) caster sugar
* 6 medium eggs
* Few drops vanilla extract
* 3tbsp milk
* 100g bar white chocolate, melted
* 100g bar milk chocolate, melted
* 100g bar dark chocolate, melted

FOR THE GANACHE:
* 300ml carton whipping cream
* 200g bar dark chocolate, broken into pieces
* Few drops vanilla extract
* White chocolate stars, for decoration

* 3 x 20cm (8in) round sandwich cake tins, buttered, floured and base-lined

1 Set the oven to 190°C or Gas Mark 5. Tip the butter, flour, sugar, eggs, vanilla extract and milk into a bowl and beat well until smooth. Divide the mixture evenly between 3 bowls. Stir the white chocolate into one of the bowls and spoon it out into a cake tin and spread out. Stir the milk chocolate into another portion and spoon into another tin and stir the dark chocolate into the final portion, then spread it out in the last tin.

2 Place the cakes in the oven, with 2 on the upper shelf and 1 on lower shelf. Bake the cakes for 25-30 minutes until they have risen and feel just firm to the touch. The cake on the bottom shelf may need an extra 5 minutes as, depending on the oven, it may not cook as quickly as the top ones. Remove from the oven and leave to cool in the tins for about 5 minutes, then transfer to a wire rack and cool completely.

3 To make the ganache: Bring the cream to the boil and pour it over the chocolate. Stir until chocolate melts and mix well, preferably using a stick blender. Stir in vanilla extract to taste. Leave the mixture to cool. Once cold, whisk the ganache until it's a spreading consistency.

4 Place the white chocolate cake on a serving plate and spread some ganache on the top, then place the milk chocolate cake on top. Spread some ganache over that, then place the dark chocolate cake on top. Spread the remaining ganache over the top and sides of the cake. Sprinkle over some white chocolate stars. Keep the cake in a cool place until serving.

※ **To freeze: The cake layers can be packed individually in freezer bags and frozen for up to 3 months. Allow them to defrost before assembling the cake with the ganache. Do not freeze the complete cake.**

Tip from our kitchen

When making the cake, if you mix the white chocolate in first, then the milk chocolate and finally the dark chocolate, you can use the same spatula for all the mixing without having to wash it in between the different flavours.

Click

He'd been distant ever since she'd landed her new job. He called his sudden change of attitude their two-year blip, as though he was an expert on blips...

'It's a blip,' Rob had said, days before. 'We'll fix it.'

Like a dripping tap, their relationship needed a new washer. Jill lay in bed, counting the tissues on the floor. 'Nineteen, twenty,' she muttered in a throaty rumble. 'What do you do all day?' she launched at Rob as, across the room, he hauled on his faded jeans and a ripped T-shirt. She sat up in bed, her hands clamped around a mug, the steam from a hot lemon drink drifting into her blocked sinuses. 'Who are you?'

'It's your cold making you like this,' he replied. 'You have a fever.'

'No, really, Rob. There's this huge big hole of time when you just disappear.'

He leaned over the duvet, one big calloused hand landing on her forehead. 'Do we have a thermometer anywhere?'

She pulled her head away. 'I'm interested.'

He headed for the door, shaking his tousled head all the way. 'No, you're not. I'm a brickie, Jill. I build houses. I have done since I left school. You're smart enough to guess the rest.'

Slam! The front door rattled in its frame when he left that morning. He'd been distant ever since she'd landed her new job. He called his sudden change of attitude a blip. 'It's our two-year blip,' he'd say, as if he was an expert on blips.

'Twenty-one.' Jill blew her nose, then threw another tissue on the floor. The bin was full. She ought to empty it. She lay back into her pillow and stared at the ceiling. Did Rob hate the fact his job might not be hard to imagine? Did he find it hard to imagine her new one? Should she have explained?

She pushed the duvet back and climbed out of bed. She rested one hand on her forehead, her head thumping as she leaned over and swept the tissues into a big pile. 'Tissue mountain,' she thought. 'Tissue Ben Nevis.'

She reached for her mobile on the bedside table. Maybe that would make Rob laugh?

She snapped a picture of tissue Ben Nevis and sent it to him. *Mountain out of a tissue molehill,* her message read. *Sorry.*

He'd still be driving to the building site. He wouldn't reply.

She'd told him her new job wasn't highbrow, just full to the brim with routine. Yet every time she mentioned it he seemed to shrug into himself.

'So you're going to work in a research laboratory now?' he'd said when her acceptance letter had first arrived. 'You're off to be a mad scientist?'

'I'm a laboratory technician,' Jill thought, as she sagged down on the edge of the bed, her phone in her hand. 'I do tests and analyse results. It's methodical and precise.

> 'Tissue mountain,' she thought. 'Tissue Ben Nevis'

I build results, Rob; you build houses. What on earth is there to get upset about?'

Her phone beeped.

He'd sent her a picture of the building site. Three half-built houses were in shot, smothered in scaffolding. Here it is, was his message. *My big black hole.*

She frowned. Was that sarcasm? Did he really feel that inadequate?

She sent him a picture of her empty bed. *Getting up now.*

Me too – a picture returned of a ladder leading skyward.

In the kitchen she snapped a picture of the breakfast dishes. *My pile of dishes. My pile of bricks* came back.

He really got into taking snaps after that, sending views from his scaffolding perch of rolling hills basked in bright summer sunlight, his mate Gary's big grinning face, the straight line of the wall he was building. She could feel his pride in that photo. *I made this.* He really did make homes from the ground floor up. He fashioned windows and doors for them.

Wow! she sent back.

His picture-sending ceased then for half an hour.

I mean it, Rob, it's fabulous what you do, she sent, as the silence lingered on and on. Did she sound patronising? *I mean it,* she repeated. *Why don't you think that I do?*

Another long pause...and he replied with a picture of a fully-completed house. Actually, it looked about the size of a small mansion. His message read: *This is what I helped make last week. I suppose it is pretty amazing, isn't it? When did I forget that?*

About the time I landed my new job? Jill thought. She wiped her eyes, tissue Ben Nevis gaining a taller summit. Had she just found the right-sized washer to fix their dripping tap, the washer that would stop Rob leaking confidence and all his manly self-esteem?

Yes, Rob. It is amazing. Now show me some more.

* * *

Jill sighed at Rob as he lay surrounded by tissues a few days later. They'd shared their cold. That seemed apt. 'He's going to make a tissue mountain the size of Everest later,' she thought, as she hurried to the door. From there, she waved her phone at him.

He smiled. 'I can't wait to see what my mad scientist does all day,' he said, sounding bunged-up and nasal – but happy.

'I promise to introduce you to all my Petri dishes,' she said.

He'd asked her to send photos of her first day back at work. She hadn't suggested it. He wanted her to feel proud of what she did, too. That was when she knew they were back on track. Their crisis was over, peace and harmony had been restored. Their blip had disappeared as fast as the click of a camera phone.

THE END
© Jo Styles, 2013

23 Monday

24 Tuesday

25 Wednesday

26 Thursday

27 Friday

28 Saturday

1 Sunday

Easy-peasy

A Bit More Tricky

Hard-ish

Quite A Challenge

Flattering
Frill

This elegant design, knitted in a fine-weight yarn, will flatter every shape

MEASUREMENTS

To fit sizes 76 (81) (86) (91) (97) (102) (107) cm/30 (32) (34) (36) (38) (40) (42) in.

Actual measurements 82.5 (88) (93.5) (99) (104) (110) (115.5) cm/ 32½ (34½) (36¾) (39) (41) (43¼) (45½) in.

Side seam including edging All sizes 49cm/19¼in.

Length to back neck, including edging 70 (70.5) (71) (73) (74) (74.5) (76) cm/27½ (27¾) (28) (28¾) (29) (29¼) (30) in.

Sleeve seam 32 (32) (32) (33) (33) (33) (34) cm/12½ (12½) (12½) (13) (13) (13) (13½) in.

MATERIALS

5 (5) (6) (6) (6) (6) (7) x 50g hanks of Manos del Uruguay Fair Trade Serena (60% baby alpaca, 40% prima cotton) in Azure (2500). Pair of 3mm (No. 11), 3¼mm (No. 10) and 4mm (No. 8) knitting needles. For yarn stockists, write to: Artesano, Unit G, Lamb's Farm Business Park, Basingstoke Road, Swallowfield, Reading, Berkshire RG7 1PQ. Call 0118 950 3350, or visit artesanoyarns.co.uk

TENSION

22 stitches and 30 rows to 10 x 10cm, over stocking stitch, using 4mm needles.

ABBREVIATIONS

K, knit; **p**, purl; **st**, stitch; **sl**, slip; **tog**, together; **k2togb**, k2tog through back of sts; **dec**, decrease (by taking 2 sts tog); **inc**, increase (by working twice in same st); **yf**, yarn forward to make a st; **nil**, meaning nothing is worked here for this size; **ss**, stocking st (k on right side, p on wrong side).

NOTE

Yarn amounts are based on average requirements and are therefore approximate. Instructions are given for small size. Where they vary, work figures in round brackets for larger sizes. Instructions in square brackets are worked as stated after 2nd bracket.

BACK

With 4mm needles, cast on 99 (105) (111) (117) (123) (129) (135) sts. Beginning with a k row, ss 2 rows.
1st eyelet row: K7, [yf, k2togb, k4] to last 8 sts, yf, k2togb, k6.
Beginning with a p row, ss 5 rows.
2nd eyelet row: K4, [yf, k2togb, k4] to last 5 sts, yf, k2togb, k3.
Beginning with a p row, ss 5 rows. Work 1st eyelet row again.
Beginning with a p row, ss 7 rows.
Dec row: K15, k2togb, k to last 17 sts, k2tog, k15. Ss 11 rows. Repeat last 12 rows, twice more, then work dec row again – 91 (97) (103) (109) (115) (121) (127) sts.
Ss another 41 rows.
Shape raglan armholes: Cast off 3 (3) (3) (3) (3) (5) (5) sts at beginning of next 2 rows.
Dec row: K2, k2togb, k to last 4 sts, k2tog, k2. Ss 3 rows.
Repeat last 4 rows, 3 (2) (1) (1) (nil) (nil) (nil) time(s) more – 77 (85) (93) (99) (107) (109) (115) sts.
Next dec row: K2, k2togb, k to last 4 sts, k2tog, k2. P 1 row. Repeat last 2 rows, 21 (24) (28) (30) (33) (34) (36) times more – 33 (35) (35) (37) (39) (39) (41) sts.
Leave remaining sts on a spare needle.

FRONT

With 4mm needles, cast on 99 (105) (111) (117) (123) (129) (135) sts. Beginning with a k row, ss 2 rows.
1st eyelet row: K7, [yf, k2togb, k4] to last 8 sts, yf, k2togb, k6.
Beginning with a p row, ss 5 rows.
2nd eyelet row: K4, [yf, k2togb, k4] to last 5 sts, yf, k2togb, k3.
Beginning with a p row, ss 5 rows. Work 1st eyelet row again.
Beginning with a p row, ss 7 rows.
Dec row: K15, k2togb, k to last 17 sts, k2tog, k15. Ss 11 rows. Repeat last 12 rows, twice more, then work dec row again – 91 (97) (103) (109) (115) (121) (127) sts.
Ss another 41 rows.
Shape raglan armholes: Cast off 3 (3) (3) (3) (3) (5) (5) sts at beginning of next 2 rows.
Dec row: K2, k2togb, k to last 4 sts, k2tog, k2. Ss 3 rows. Repeat last 4 rows, 3 (2) (1) (1) (nil) (nil) (nil) time(s) more – 77 (85) (93) (99) (107) (109) (115) sts.

Next dec row: K2, k2togb, k to last 4 sts, k2tog, k2. P 1 row. Repeat last 2 rows, 13 (16) (19) (21) (23) (24) (25) times more – 49 (51) (53) (55) (59) (59) (63) sts.
Shape neck: Next row: K2, k2togb, k10 (10) (11) (11) (12) (12) (13), turn and work on these 13 (13) (14) (14) (15) (15) (16) sts only for left side.
Left side: 1st dec row: P2tog, p to end. **2nd dec row:** K2, k2togb, k to last 2 sts, k2tog. Repeat last 2 rows, once more – 7 (7) (8) (8) (9) (9) (10) sts. P 1 row.
Next dec row: K2, k2togb, k to end. P 1 row. Repeat last 2 rows, 2 (2) (3) (3) (4) (4) (5) times more – 4 sts.
Next dec row: K2, k2togb. P 1 row.
Next dec row: K1, k2togb. P 1 row.
Next dec row: K2togb. Fasten off.
Right side: With right side facing, slip centre 21 (23) (23) (25) (27) (27) (29) sts on to a stitch holder, rejoin yarn to remaining sts and k to last 4 sts, k2tog, k2 – 13 (13) (14) (14) (15) (15) (16) sts.
1st dec row: P to last 2 sts, p2tog. **2nd dec row:** K2tog, k to last 4 sts, k2tog, k2. Repeat last 2 rows, once more – 7 (7) (8) (8) (9) (9) (10) sts. P 1 row.
Next dec row: K to last 4 sts, k2tog, k2. P 1 row. Repeat last 2 rows, 2 (2) (3) (3) (4) (4) (5) times more – 4 sts.
Next dec row: K2tog, k2. P 1 row.
Next dec row: K2tog, k1. P 1 row.
Next dec row: K2tog. Fasten off.

SLEEVES (both alike)

With 3¼mm needles, cast on 48 (50) (52) (54) (58) (60) (62) sts.
K 5 rows, increasing 1 st at each end of last row – 50 (52) (54) (56) (60) (62) (64) sts.
Change to 4mm needles.
Beginning with a k row, ss 6 rows.
Inc 1 st at each end of next row and 6 (7) (8) (9) (10) (11) (12) following 12th (10th) (9th) (8th) (7th) (7th) (6th) rows – 64 (68) (72) (76) (82) (86) (90) sts.
Ss another 13 (15) (13) (15) (17) (10) (19) rows.
Shape raglan top: Cast off 3 (3) (3) (3) (3) (5) (5) sts at beginning of next 2 rows.
Dec row: K2, k2togb, k to last 4 sts, k2tog, k2. Ss 3 rows.
Repeat last 4 rows, 3 (2) (2) (2) (1) (2) (2) time(s) more – 50 (56) (60) (64) (72) (70) (74) sts.

Next dec row: K2, k2togb, k to last 4 sts, k2tog, k2. P 1 row. Repeat last 2 rows, 21 (24) (26) (28) (31) (30) (32) times more – 6 (6) (6) (6) (8) (8) (8) sts.
Leave remaining sts on a st holder.

NECKBAND

Join both front and right back raglan seams.
With right side facing and using 3¼mm needles, work across left sleeve top thus: k4 (4) (4) (4) (6) (6) (6), k2tog, pick up and k13 (13) (15) (15) (17) (17) (19) sts down left front neck, k21 (23) (23) (25) (27) (27) (29) sts across centre front, pick up and k13 (13) (15) (15) (17) (17) (19) sts up right front neck, work across right sleeve top thus: k2togb, k2 (2) (2) (2) (4) (4) (4), k2tog, finally work across back neck thus: k2tog, k31 (33) (33) (35) (37) (37) (39) – 88 (92) (96) (100) (112) (112) (120) sts. K 4 rows.
Change to 3mm needles and k 4 rows. With 4mm needles, cast off kwise.

HEM EDGING

With 4mm needles, cast on 22 sts.
1st row: Sl1, k1, [yf, k2tog] 9 times, yf, k2 - 23 sts. **2nd row and every alternate row:** K. **3rd row:** Sl1, k4, [yf, k2tog] 8 times, yf, k2 – 24 sts. **5th row:** Sl1, k7, [yf, k2tog] 7 times, yf, k2 – 25 sts. **7th row:** Sl1, k10, [yf, k2tog] 6 times, yf, k2 – 26 sts. **9th row:** Sl1, k13, [yf, k2tog] 5 times, yf, k2 – 27 sts. **11th row:** Sl1, k16, [yf, k2tog] 4 times, yf, k2 – 28 sts. **13th row:** Sl1, k19, [yf, k2tog] 3 times, yf, k2 – 29 sts. **15th row:** Sl1, k22, [yf, k2tog] twice, yf, k2 – 30 sts. **17th row:** Sl1, k25, yf, k2tog, yf, k2 – 31 sts.
9th row: Sl1, k to end. **20th row:** Cast off 9 sts loosely, k to end – 22 sts. These 20 rows form pattern.
Continue in pattern until straight edge of edging fits along lower edge of back and front, taking care not to stretch edging and ending with 19th pattern row. Cast off.

TO MAKE UP

Join left back raglan seam and neckband. Join side and sleeve seams. Beginning at side seam, sew straight edge of hem edging along lower edge of back and front. Join cast-on and cast-off edges together, working to within 9 sts from point on cast-off edge.

Making Your
Garden Grow

Got a few minutes (or an hour) to spare? Choose from Adrienne Wild's prepare-for-summer jobs

If you only have...

5 Minutes

Cover strawberries with cloches for an early crop.

10 Minutes

Tidy weather-worn patio containers. Pick off fading flowers and foliage and trim back any frost-damaged shoots. Replace dead plants.

Sow French beans in a windowsill propagator for early crops.

30 Minutes

Clean out water butts ready for the spring rains. Add Biotal Refresh or potassium permanganate to the water to keep it clean. Add a tight-fitting lid to keep out debris.

Cut back the old foliage on ornamental grasses.

Prune *Jasminum nudiflorum* after flowering to encourage new growth for next year's blooms. Cut back the previous year's growth to 5cm from the old wood.

Cut shrubs that flower in summer on new-season growth (such as buddleja) hard, to encourage plenty of new shoots.

45 Minutes

Plant shrubs to frame the boundary of the garden and give the impression of hidden depth. Where space is limited, clothe the walls with climbers to achieve a similar effect.

60 Minutes

Clean paths and patios to instantly improve the overall appearance of your garden. Hire a pressure washer for tough dirt; use chemical path and decking cleaners on algae.

15 Minutes

BUY pot-ready flower and vegetable seedlings from the garden centre and grow them on the windowsill indoors. Water them with pbi Cheshunt Compound to reduce the risk of them damping off.

MARCH

POST – CARD

Reader Janet Trevellyan nominates Mo'orea, French Polynesia, in the South Pacific

'I visited Moorea, near Tahiti, after surviving a life-threatening illness, and stayed in a thatched bungalow, surrounded by sweet-perfumed flowers and birdsong. I cycled around in my sarong, walked barefoot at the water's edge, swam, chatted with the locals and walked the forests. The highlight of my trip was a traditional Polynesian feast, with dancers entertaining us long into the night.'

2 Monday

3 Tuesday

4 Wednesday

5 Thursday

6 Friday

7 Saturday

8 Sunday

Asian Stir-Fry

Serves 2-3	
Calories: 408	
Fat: 14g	
Saturated fat: 3g	
Suitable for freezing: ✗	

* Zest and juice of 1 lime
* 4 tablespoons teriyaki sauce
* 2 skinned salmon fillets, about 125g (4oz) each
* 2 nests of dried medium egg noodles
* 300g pack colourful stir-fry veg mix

TO SERVE:
* Soy sauce

1 Mix the lime zest with the teriyaki sauce in a small, shallow dish. Add the salmon, coat the pieces well, then leave to marinate for 10 minutes.

2 Heat a wok or pan over a medium heat, then add 1 tablespoon vegetable oil. Scrape excess marinade from the salmon, then add the fish to the pan and fry for 2-3 minutes on each side, until just cooked. Take it out of the pan and set aside.

3 Cook the noodles as instructed on the pack. Meanwhile, add the leftover marinade from the dish to the wok with the veg, and stir-fry for 3-4 minutes.

4 Add the drained noodles to the wok and mix in. Top with large flakes of salmon.

5 Sprinkle with lime juice and serve hot, with soy sauce to taste.

Tip from our kitchen

Add some fresh coriander leaves for extra flavour. You can make this with chicken or beef strips.

Your Good Health

Ask Dr Mel

Q I may need a hip replacement, but I'd like to wait until I retire – does it make sense to delay the operation until then?

A Many factors could influence your decision. Obviously the most important one is how far your osteoarthritis has advanced – it usually progresses slowly, so you may not need surgery for many years (if ever). It also depends on how much the pain, stiffness and reduced mobility are affecting your daily activities and sleep, and whether/how long these symptoms can be improved by weight loss, painkillers, physiotherapy, a walking aid and/or a steroid injection.

You also need to consider what you're hoping to do before and after you retire, whether your general health might deteriorate, making surgery more risky, and whether the NHS may ration future joint replacements. Arguments for postponing the op include the three-month recovery time, possible technical improvements in the future, and the fact you may need a second replacement hip after 10 or more years.

In the meantime, keeping your weight down can slow arthritis progression, and US researchers have recently said that education/exercise/physio programmes to increase strength, flexibility and function can delay surgery by almost two years.

TAKE 5...
Sex Problems That Can Be Remedied

1 FATIGUE caused by anaemia, underactive thyroid, diabetes, and other diseases.

2 BEING TOO BUSY or 'living online' – make time to be 'in the moment' with each other.

3 TOO MUCH ALCOHOL – it provokes the desire, but takes away the performance.

4 STRESS AND DEPRESSION (tell your doctor if antidepressants affect desire or orgasm).

5 RELATIONSHIP DIFFICULTIES – sex therapy or counselling may help (eg, Relate: call 0300 100 1234; visit relate.org.uk).

A Great Exercise To...
Firm up bingo wings

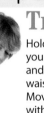

Tricep Kickbacks

Holding a 500ml bottle of water in your right hand, bend your knees and lean forwards slightly from the waist, keeping your back straight. Move your right elbow behind you, with the arm bent at 90 degrees, then straighten the arm as far behind you as is comfortable. Bend the arm forward again to return to your starting position. Repeat 10 to 15 times on each side.
Well done!

HOW THE EXPERTS STAY HEALTHY
Nita Saini, well-being author

What's in your medicine cabinet?
Vitamin C and probiotics. I take these every day. If I'm feeling run down, I'll also take echinacea drops to boost my immune system.

What's good in your fridge?
Fresh ginger and garlic. First thing, I drink a glass of hot water with grated ginger and lemon juice. And I use garlic in my cooking.

What's your favourite exercise?
A 20- to 30-minute daily routine that includes cardio (step-ups on the bottom stair), muscle-building exercises for the arms and legs, ab crunches and some stretches. Three times a week I go for a 20-minute walk, too.

What's a special treat?
A bar of Green & Black's dark chocolate.

How do you cope with stress?
I do deep abdominal breathing. It slows everything down and stops my mind racing. Also BETOP – 'Believing Everything Turns Out Perfect'.

Do you have any childhood remedies that still work?
Heinz Organic Tomato Soup. It's really warming and nurturing when I'm feeling a bit poorly.

● *Moving On Up! Secrets To An Upbeat And Happy Life* by Nita Saini (Jayra UK, £8.99). For a free de-stressing, uplifting audio, visit movingonupthebook.com

9 Monday

10 Tuesday

11 Wednesday

12 Thursday

13 Friday

14 Saturday

15 Sunday

Your Handmade Easter

Egg-stra special makes to spread seasonal cheer around your home

Bristle chick, a selection, C Graham. Boc Oliver Bonas

Bags Of Fun

You will need

FOR EACH BAG:
- 2 pieces of 15 x 11cm felt in pink, white or blue
- Ribbons and ric rac
- Threads and pins
- Scissors and ruler

Craft tip

This is a great project for using up any old scraps of ribbons and fabrics.

1 Lay the two pieces of felt flat and pin 11cm strips of ribbon or ric rac at intervals across the width of each, as above. Use a ruler to ensure each ribbon is straight and lines up on both pieces.

2 Sew the ribbons/ric rac on to the felt – thin ribbons and ric rac will only need one line of stitching, but thicker ones will need to be secured at both edges, so they don't flap open.

3 Place the felt pieces together, ribbon sides facing, and sew around the two edges and along the bottom edge.

4 For the handle, cut a 25cm length of ribbon and sew it to either side of the top of the bag.

● *Felt, ribbons and ric rac, all from a selection at Hobbycraft (0330 026 1400; hobbycraft.co.uk)*

Crack It

To make a cute egg vase, carefully crack off the top of an egg with a teaspoon. Pour out the yolk and white, and rinse thoroughly. Leave to dry, select your prettiest egg cups (ours are from a selection at John Lewis) and arrange your flowers. Tiny, delicate sprays work well.

Message In A Bottle

Photos: Susie Bell, Styling: Emily Dawe, assisted by Sophie Bellenberg. Bottle covers and ribbon tags by Emma Morton-Turner

You will need

- 6 empty wine (or similar) bottles
- 70cm of 115cm-wide cotton
- 20cm lace ribbon per bottle
- Assorted ribbons
- Alphabet stencil
- Scrap of card
- Fabric paints
- Paintbrush
- Masking tape
- Scissors and pen
- Threads
- Sewing machine

Craft tip

Don't sew together the bottom of the covers. If left open, they will sit neatly flat to the shape of the bottle.

1 Lay your bottle on the fabric, draw round it with a pen, adding 4cm all round for seam allowance. Cut two pieces the same size for one bottle. (We used wine bottles, but you can use any size you like.)

2 Lay the two pieces of fabric, right sides together, then pin and sew along the long edges. Press the seams flat. Turn through to the right side.

3 Turn the top and bottom edges up 1cm, sew the hem in place and press with an iron.

4 Place a piece of card inside the cover to prevent the paint seeping through the fabric, then position your alphabet stencil using masking tape.

5 To use a stencil successfully on fabric, the trick is to apply paint to the paintbrush, then remove most of it on kitchen paper. Make a stabbing action over the stencil until each letter is complete – this prevents paint seeping underneath, and also helps it dry quickly if you want to give it a second coat.

6 Let the paint dry before you sew lace on to the top of the cover and ribbon to the bottom. Slip the cover over the bottle, tie some ribbon round the neck and place on your mantelpiece or on the centre of the table. Repeat for each bottle.

● *Fabric, fabric paints, lace ribbon, all from a selection at Hobbycraft (hobbycraft.co.uk). Alphabet stencil, from a selection at The Stencil Library (stencil-library.com). Cordial bottles, from a selection at Lakeland (lakeland.co.uk). Ribbons, from a selection at Jane Means (janemeans.co.uk)*

Other Women

All my friends had a mum. I just had a dad who seemed like a stranger

You could never have looked at us and said who was at fault, even though I grew up feeling a nuisance, and just another worry for my dad. He did his best, but he had to work, and while he was working, I was wandering around on the outside of my friends' lives, wishing I had a mum like them and longing to feel part of a family.

But I didn't have a family any more. Mum died when I was seven, and sometimes I panicked because I couldn't remember her face. Other times, I caught a whiff of lavender soap and just for a moment, she was back, and I had a wonderful feeling of warm arms and a soft kiss. She used to laugh a lot, and tease me, and sometimes, if I'd been particularly good, I remember she'd find a chocolate, hidden under a pillow, or stashed behind a coffee jar.

'Goodness Katy, look what I've found,' she'd say, and hand it over.

The house was never the same after that. It always seemed cold and empty. Dad worked even at weekends, and sometimes, when he looked at me, I had the feeling he wanted to run. He'd turn and leave the room. I never knew why he was like that and I grew up feeling I didn't belong anywhere. I wished Dad liked me a bit, but he always seemed to be dreaming of somewhere else. Sometimes, I'd show him my homework, and he'd glance at it and say very nice, but I could tell he wasn't interested, so I stopped bothering.

I heard a neighbour once, talking to her friend at the gate, about Dad. She said something about him still missing Mum.

'Not easy for a man on his own,' she said, and I wanted to scream. I wanted to shake her, and tell her my dad wasn't on his own, he had me, and I loved him but he didn't care. Two years on, Dad was a stranger. Moody and distant, he hardly spoke to me at all. Then things began to change. He stopped sitting around staring into space and began sprucing himself up a bit. He started going out, and getting home late, and sometimes, I'd see him smiling to himself and wish he'd smile at me like that. After a while, he brought Hilary home. He'd told me about her, and I'd clammed up completely. The day I met her, I wanted to die. When she moved in, I longed to move out, but I couldn't. I stayed out late, crashed around the house, or stayed in my room refusing to talk to her. I think she tried quite hard to begin with, but eventually, she gave up, and thinking back on it, I can understand why she became so cool towards me. Dad said I should try harder, and I wanted to shout at him. I wanted to scream, 'Well, you didn't try very hard with me,' but I didn't, just went into my room and slammed the door. I felt even more of an outsider.

I think we were all relieved when I went to uni. I got a decent degree, and met Dave. Suddenly, I was loved. Someone in my world said I was special. He said he couldn't imagine life without me, and I felt the same about him. And as the years went on, things got even better when our baby was born and we became a proper family. Dad looked as pleased as punch to be a grandfather and gave me a hug with tears in his eyes. I just wished I could keep everything exactly as it was, but nothing stays the same does it?

Deep down, I knew it would happen one day. They say people change every seven years, so I've been luckier than some. I've been the most important woman in his life for most of that time and I've never been so happy. But recently I've noticed a change. When I think about it, I shake myself, tell myself this is life, so I'd better get used to it. But just for a moment, I'm lost, grieving at time passing, and the way the years show themselves on my face and in my outlook on life. And even though he doesn't realise this yet, I know he's met another woman, one who's younger, more vibrant, and in touch with things that are so important to him at present.

I've seen her several times. She laughs a lot, she's pretty in an outdoor sort of way, and radiates the sort of vitality that's the prerogative of the late teens. That halcyon point in our lives when we know, absolutely, we're just a few steps away from conquering the world. I can see why he's so captivated.

At first, when I dropped him off at his meetings, he'd turn and wave before he disappeared. And when it was time to pick him up, he'd be outside, waiting. Always, the moment he saw me, he'd give me the full force of his wonderful smile. That no longer happens. He barely says thank you before he races away, and he's always the last one out after the meeting, feet dragging, looking back, reluctant to leave. He's found a whole new world in her, and he hates to leave it.

He never used to care too much about the way he looked. He'd run his fingers through his hair, fling on a jacket and be ready to go. This evening, his hair is brushed, his shoes polished, and his new woodcraft badge is sewn on perfectly.

'It looks wonderful,' I say.

'Thanks,' he says, and we're off. Akela's at the door this evening, shepherding in her cub scouts. They all look up to her, and adore her. For the moment, my son has a new woman in his life, and doesn't look back as he rushes to meet her.

I drive back home and Dave's there, waiting for me.

'Coffee,' he says and smiles. The wonderful smile his son has inherited, along with his sense of fun and kind, loving nature.

'Tom's growing up fast,' he says, and I nod and give him a kiss.

'He's finding the world outside.' I smile. 'Just as long as he grows up like his dad,' I add. And send up a little word of thanks for all the good things in my life.

THE END

© Sheila Alcock, 2013

> *I grew up feeling I didn't belong anywhere*

16 Monday

17 Tuesday

18 Wednesday

19 Thursday

20 Friday

21 Saturday

22 Sunday

Serene In Cerise

Wrap up your little one in this bright, chunky cable hoodie

MEASUREMENTS

To fit ages 3-6 (6-9) (9-12) (12-18) months.

Actual measurements 55.5 (59) (62) (66) cm/21¾ (23¼) (24½) (26) in.

Side seam 15.5 (17) (19) (21) cm/ 6 (6¾) (7½) (8¼) in.

Length to back neck 27 (29.5) (32) (35) cm/10½ (11½) (12½) (13¾) in.

Sleeve seam 17 (19) (21) (23) cm/6¾ (7½) (8¼) (9) in.

MATERIALS

6 (9) 50g balls of Sublime Baby Cashmere Merino Silk DK (75% merino, 20% silk, 5% cashmere) in Pinkaboo (162). Size 4.00 crochet hook. You can buy the yarn online at womansweeklyshop.com/yarn or call 0800 024 1212.

TENSION

19 stitches and 23 rows, to 10 x 10cm, over double crochet pattern, using 4.00 hook.

ABBREVIATIONS

Ch, chain; **st**, stitch; **dc**, double crochet; **slst**, slip st; **nil**, meaning nothing is worked here for this size; **dec**, decrease; **dc2tog**, [insert hook in next st, yarn over hook and draw through] twice, yarn over hook and draw through all 3 loops on hook.

NOTE

Yarn amounts are based on average requirements and are therefore approximate. Instructions are given for small size. Where they vary, work figures in round brackets for larger sizes. Instructions in square brackets are worked as stated after 2nd bracket.

BACK

With 4.00 hook, make 54 (57) (60) (64) ch.

Foundation row (right side): 1dc in 2nd ch from hook (counts as 1 st), [1dc in next ch] to end, turn – 53 (56) (59) (63) dc.

Pattern row: 1ch (does not count as a st), 1dc in first dc, [1dc in next dc] to end, turn.

Pattern another 34 (38) (42) (46) rows. **

Shape armholes: Next row: Slst into each of first 4 sts, 1ch (does not count as a st), 1dc in same dc as last slst, [1dc in next dc] to last 3dc, turn.

Dec row: 1ch (does not count as a st), dc2tog, pattern to last 2dc, dc2tog, turn.

Repeat dec row, 4 times more – 37 (40) (43) (47) dc.

Pattern another 20 (22) (24) (26) rows.

Fasten off.

FRONT

Work as back to **.

Shape armhole and neck: Dividing row: Slst into first 4 sts, 1ch (does not count as a st), 1dc in same dc as last slst, [1dc in next dc] 17 (18) (19) (21) times, turn and work on these 18 (19) (20) (22) sts only for left side.

Left side: 1st dec row: Pattern to last 2dc, dc2tog, turn.

2nd dec row: 1ch (does not count as a st), dc2tog, pattern to end.

Repeat last 2 rows, once more – 14 (15) (16) (18) dc.

3rd dec row: 1ch (does not count as a st), dc2tog, pattern to last 2dc, dc2tog, turn.

Pattern 3 rows. Work 2nd dec row.

Repeat last 4 rows, 2 (2) (2) (3) times more – 9 (10) (11) (12) dc.

Pattern another 8 (10) (12) (10) rows.

Fasten off.

Right side: With right side facing, return to end of dividing row, miss next 11 (12) (13) (13) sts, join yarn to

next st with slst, 1ch (does not count as a st), 1dc in same dc as slst, [1dc in next dc] to last 3dc, turn – 18 (19) (20) (22) dc.

1st dec row: 1ch (does not count as a st), dc2tog, pattern to end.

2nd dec row: Pattern to last 2dc, dc2tog, turn.

Repeat last 2 rows, once more – 14 (15) (16) (18) dc.

3rd dec row: 1ch (does not count as a st), dc2tog, pattern to last 2dc, dc2tog, turn.

Pattern 3 rows. Work 2nd dec row.

Repeat last 4 rows, 2 (2) (2) (3) times more – 9 (10) (11) (12) dc.

Pattern another 8 (10) (12) (10) rows.

Fasten off.

SLEEVES (both alike)

With 4.00 hook, make 31 (33) (35) (37) ch.

Foundation row (right side): 1dc in 2nd ch from hook (counts as 1 st), [1dc in next ch] to end, turn – 30 (32) (34) (36) dc.

Pattern row: 1ch (does not count as a st), 1dc in first dc, [1dc in next dc] to end, turn.

Pattern another 2 rows.

Increase row: 1ch (does not count as a st), 2dc in first dc, pattern to last dc, 2dc in last dc, turn. Pattern another 7 rows.

Repeat last 8 rows, 3 (3) (4) (4) times more, then work increase row again – 40 (42) (46) (48) dc. Pattern another 3 (7) (3) (9) rows.

Shape top: Next row: Slst into each of first 4 sts, 1ch (does not count as a st), 1dc in same dc as last slst, [1dc in next dc] to last 3dc, turn.

Dec row: 1ch (does not count as a st), dc2tog, pattern to last 2dc, dc2tog, turn. Pattern 1 row.

Repeat last 2 rows, 4 (5) (5) (6) times more – 24 (24) (28) (28) dc.

Repeat dec row, 7 (7) (9) (9) times more – 10dc. Fasten off.

HOOD

Join shoulder seams.

First half: With 4.00 hook, make 20 (22) (24) (26) ch for back edge.

Foundation row (right side): 1dc in 2nd ch from hook (counts as 1 st), [1dc in next ch] to end, turn – 19 (21) (23) (25) dc.

1st row: 1ch (does not count as a st), 2dc in first dc, [1dc in next dc] to end, 5ch, turn.

2nd row: 1dc in 2nd ch from hook, 1dc in each of next 3ch, [1dc in next dc] to last dc, 2dc in last dc, turn. Repeat last 2 rows, once more, then work 1st row again.

6th row: 1dc in 2nd ch from hook, 1dc in each of next 3ch, [1dc in next dc] to end, turn. **7th row:** 1ch (does not count as a st), 1dc in first dc, [1dc in next dc] to end, 5ch, turn.

8th row: As 6th row – 40 (42) (44) (46) dc.

Fasten off.

Second half: With 4.00 hook, make 20 (22) (24) (26) ch for back edge.

Foundation row (right side): 1dc in 2nd ch from hook (counts as 1 st), [1dc in next ch] to end, turn – 19 (21) (23) (25) dc.

1st row: 1ch (does not count as a st), [1dc in next dc] to last dc, 2dc in last dc, turn.

2nd row: With separate length of yarn make 4ch and leave these sts, 1ch (does not count as a st), 2dc in first dc, [1dc in next dc] to end, then work 1dc in each ch across the 4ch, turn. Repeat last 2 rows once more, then work 1st row again.

6th row: With separate length of yarn make 4ch and leave these sts, 1ch (does not count as a st), 1dc in first dc, [1dc in next dc] to end, then work 1dc in each ch across the 4ch, turn. **7th row:** 1ch (does not count as a st), [1dc in next dc] to end, turn.

8th row: As 6th row – 40 (42) (44) (46) dc.

Joining row: Pattern 38 (40) (42) (44), 2dc in next dc, 1dc in next dc, then work across first half thus: 1dc in first dc, 2dc in next dc, pattern to end – 82 (86) (90) (94) dc. Pattern 7 rows.

Increase row: Pattern to within 2 sts of centre, 2dc in next dc, 1dc in each of next 2dc, 2dc in next dc, pattern to end.

Easy-peasy

A Bit More Tricky

Hard-ish

Quite A Challenge

Repeat last 8 rows, 1 (1) (2) (2) time(s) more – 86 (90) (96) (100) sts. Pattern 4 (6) (nil) (2) rows. Fasten off. Fold hood in half and join back seam. Sew row-ends of hood to back neck, easing in fullness.

Neck and hood border: With right side facing, rejoin yarn at base of front opening, 1ch (does not count as a st), 1dc in each row-end along right side neck, now work 1dc in each dc along straight edge of hood, then work 1dc in each row-end of

left side neck, turn – 138 (146) (156) (164) dc.

Pattern 2 (nil) (5) (3) rows. Pattern 1 row increasing 1 st at each side of centre 2 sts as before – 140 (148) (158) (166) sts. Pattern another 9 (13) (9) (11) rows. Fasten off.

TO MAKE UP

Lap row-ends of neck and hood border over at base of neck opening and sew in place. Sew in sleeves. Join side and sleeve seams.

Sudoku 1

To solve this puzzle, fill in the grid so that each 3 x 3 box, each row and each column contains the numbers 1-9.

You can work it out...

	6							
	1	4		8		5		
5				9	1			8
	8	6			7			
						8	2	5
				2			6	
7						9		4
4						1		2	5
		5	3				1	

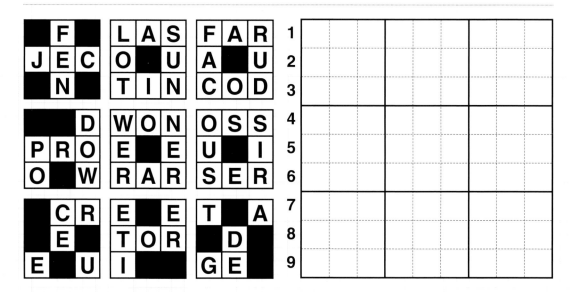

Pieceword

Using the across clues to help you, transfer the jigsaw pieces into the blank grid to form a crossword that is symmetrical from top to bottom and left to right.

ACROSS
1 Opposite of 'first' • A long way off
3 Hint of colour • Popular fish
5 Cinema machine
7 Was victorious • Annoyed
9 Lightly cooked • One who consumes or operates

Solutions to this month's puzzle on June puzzles

SOLUTIONS FOR JANUARY 2015

Answer: SKYLARK.

23 Monday

24 Tuesday

25 Wednesday

26 Thursday

27 Friday

28 Saturday

29 Sunday

APRIL

30 Monday

31 Tuesday

1 Wednesday

2 Thursday

3 Friday GOOD FRIDAY

4 Saturday

5 Sunday

Chirpy *Chicks*

Our adorable family will look great on your Easter table

MEASUREMENTS

Mother hen 17cm/6½in high and 15cm/6in long.
Chick 7cm/2¾in high.

MATERIALS

For the set: 1 x 50g ball of Rico Essential Cotton DK (100% cotton) in each of Yellow (63), Green (86) and Coral (68). Small amounts of Black DK yarn for embroidery. Pair of 3mm (No. 11) and 4mm (No. 8) knitting needles. Small amount of washable toy stuffing. You can buy the yarn online at womansweeklyshop.com/yarn or call 0800 024 1212.

TENSION

26 stitches and 36 rows, to 10 x 10cm, over stocking stitch, using 3mm needles.

ABBREVIATIONS

K, knit; **p**, purl; **st**, stitch; **tog**, together; **dec**, decrease (by taking 2 sts tog); **inc**, increase (by working twice in same st); **ss**, stocking st (k on right side and p on wrong side).

NOTE

Instructions in square brackets are worked as stated after 2nd bracket.

MOTHER HEN

BODY

With 3mm needles and Yellow, cast on 10 sts for tail end. P 1 row.
1st inc row: Inc kwise in each st – 20 sts. P 1 row.
2nd inc row: [Inc in next st, k1] to end – 30 sts. P 1 row.
3rd inc row: [Inc in next st, k2] to end – 40 sts. Ss 3 rows.
4th inc row: [Inc in next st, k3] to end – 50 sts. Ss 5 rows.
5th inc row: [Inc in next st, k4] to end – 60 sts. Ss 7 rows.
6th inc row: [Inc in next st, k5] to end – 70 sts. Ss 15 rows.
1st dec row: [K5, k2tog] to end – 60 sts. Ss 5 rows.
2nd dec row: [K4, k2tog] to end – 50 sts. Ss 3 rows. **3rd dec row:** [K3, k2tog] to end – 40 sts. P 1 row.
4th dec row: [K2, k2tog] to end – 30 sts. P 1 row.
5th dec row: [K2tog] to end – 15 sts. Break off yarn, thread end through remaining sts, pull up tightly and secure.
Gather cast-on edge, pull up tightly and secure. Join row-ends together leaving an opening. Stuff firmly and close opening.

HEAD

With 3mm needles and Yellow, cast on 10 sts. P 1 row.
1st inc row: Inc kwise in each st – 20 sts. P 1 row.
2nd inc row: [Inc in next st, k1] to end – 30 sts. Ss 17 rows.
3rd inc row: [Inc in next st, k2] to end – 40 sts. P 1 row. Cast off.

Gather cast-on edge, pull up tightly and secure.

Join row-ends together. Stuff head firmly. With seam at back, place head at front end on top of body and sew in position.

NECK TRIM

With 3mm needles and Yellow, cast on 4 sts.

Pattern row: Cast off 2 sts, place st used in casting off back on to left-hand needle and cast on 2 sts – 4 sts. Repeat pattern row, 14 times more. Cast off all sts, thus forming a ring. Place trim ring over head and sew inner edge along cast-off edge of head.

BEAK

With 3mm needles and Coral, cast on 2 sts. P 1 row.

1st inc row: Inc kwise in first st, k1 – 3 sts. P 1 row.

2nd inc row: Inc in each of first 2 sts, k1 – 5 sts. P 1 row.

3rd inc row: Inc in first st, k2, inc in next st, k1 – 7 sts. Ss 3 rows.

1st dec row: K1, k2tog, k2, k2tog – 5 sts. P 1 row.

2nd dec row: K1, [k2tog] twice – 3 sts. P 1 row.

3rd dec row: K1, k2tog – 2 sts. P2tog and fasten off.

Fold beak in half widthways and join row-ends together. Pin folded edge vertically to centre front of head and sew in position.

With Black yarn, embroider eyes either side of beak.

COMB

With 3mm needles and Green, cast on 8 sts.

Beginning with a k row, ss 2 rows.

Divide for points: * Next row: Cast off 5 sts, k to end – 3 sts.

P 1 row.

Next row: Cast on 5 sts, k to end – 8 sts. P 1 row. *

Repeat from * to *, once more.

Next row: Cast off 5 sts, place st used in casting off back on to left-hand needle and cast on 5 sts, k to end.

P 1 row.

Repeat from * to *, twice more.

Cast off all sts.

Fold comb in half, matching points and over-sew around all edges. With

folded end of comb at back, sew straight edge to top of head.

WATTLE

With 3mm needles and Green, cast on 3 sts. P 1 row.

1st inc row: Inc kwise in each of first 2 sts, k1 – 5 sts. Ss 7 rows.

Dec 1 st at beginning of next row and 2 following alternate rows – 2 sts.

P 1 row.

Inc 1 st at beginning of next row and 2 following alternate rows – 5 sts. Ss 7 rows.

Dec row: K1, [k2tog] twice – 3 sts. Cast off.

Fold wattle in half and join around all sides. Place short shaped edge vertically to centre front of head between beak and neck trim, then sew in position.

WINGS (make 2)

With 3mm needles and Green, cast on 8 sts. P 1 row.

Inc row: Inc kwise in first st, k to last 2 sts, inc in next st, k1.

Repeat last 2 rows, 3 times more – 16 sts. Ss 5 rows.

Dec 1 st at each end of next row and 6 following alternate rows – 2 sts.

P 1 row. K2tog and fasten off.

Position wings at sides of body and sew in place.

FEET (make 2)

With 3mm needles and Coral, cast on 8 sts.

Divide for digits: Next row: Cast off 6 sts, k to end – 2 sts. P 1 row.

Next row: Cast on 6 sts, cast off 6 sts, k to end. P 1 row.

Repeat last 2 rows, 3 times more. Cast on 6 sts, then cast off all sts. Fold foot in half, matching digits and over-sew around all edges. Place feet at front end of underside of body, and sew back end to body.

TAIL

With 4mm needles and Yellow, cast on 16 sts for feather.

Change to 3mm needles and cast off tightly.

Make two more, one in each of Yellow and Green.

Place Green feather between two

Yellow feathers and catch together at one short end. Place this end to back on body and sew in place.

YELLOW CHICK

BODY

With 3mm needles and Yellow, cast on 10 sts for lower edge. P 1 row.

1st inc row: Inc kwise in each st – 20 sts. P 1 row.

2nd inc row: [Inc in next st, k1] to end – 30 sts. Ss 3 rows.

3rd inc row: [Inc in next st, k2] to end – 40 sts. Ss 11 rows.

1st dec row: [K2, k2tog] to end – 30 sts. Ss 5 rows.

2nd dec row: [K1, k2tog] to end – 20 sts. P 1 row.

3rd dec row: [K2tog] to end – 10 sts. Break off yarn, thread end through remaining sts, pull up tightly and secure. Gather cast-on edge, pull up tightly and secure. Join row-ends together, leaving an opening. Stuff firmly and close opening.

BEAK

With 3mm needles and Coral, cast on 2 sts. P 1 row.

Inc row: Inc kwise in first st, k1 – 3 sts. P 1 row.

Dec row: K1, k2tog – 2 sts. P2tog and fasten off.

Fold beak in half widthways and join tiny row-ends together. Pin folded edge vertically to centre front of head just below 1st dec row and sew in position. With Black yarn, embroider eyes either side of beak.

WINGS (make 2)

With 3mm needles and Green, cast on 4 sts. P 1 row.

1st inc row: Inc kwise in first st, k to last 2 sts, inc kwise in next st, k1. P 1 row. Repeat last 2 rows, once more – 8 sts.

Dec 1 st at each end of next row and and 2 following alternate rows – 2 sts.

P 1 row. K2tog and fasten off. Position wings at sides of body and sew in place.

GREEN CHICK

Work as Yellow chick using Green instead of Yellow and vice versa.

Designer: Louise Watling

Flapper Fashion

The change in style seen between the 1910s and 1920s was as great a leap as that between the 1950s and 1960s. Femininity was out and dressing to shock was in

Inventive ideas A reader's tip from 1920 (above): a fan made from a hat feather with a cigarette holder for a handle

Waists plummet A focus on the lower half of the body still allowed plenty of fun with accessories

Fit for purpose Advances in fabrics and lifestyle changes defined women's fashion in radical new ways, but for breakfasting in a hotel, we advised wearing a hat

6 Monday EASTER MONDAY

7 Tuesday

8 Wednesday

9 Thursday

10 Friday

11 Saturday

12 Sunday

Hot Cross Buns

Makes 15
Calories per bun: 525
Fat per bun: 5g
Saturated fat: 2g
Suitable for freezing: ✗

* 500g (1lb) plain, strong white flour
* ½ teaspoon salt
* 7g sachet easy-bake dried yeast
* 2 level teaspoons mixed spice
* 1 level teaspoon ground cinnamon
* ½ teaspoon freshly grated nutmeg
* 60g (2oz) caster sugar
* 250g (8oz) mixed dried fruit
* 60g (2oz) butter
* 200ml (7fl oz) full-cream milk
* 1 large egg, beaten

FOR THE CROSSES:
* 60g (2oz) plain flour
* 1 teaspoon oil

FOR THE GLAZE:
* 60g (2oz) caster sugar

1 Put the flour into the bowl of an electric mixer fitted with a dough hook, or into a large bowl. Stir in the salt, yeast, spices, sugar and fruit.

2 Gently heat the butter in a small pan until just melted. Add the milk and heat for 1 minute, until tepid. Pour buttery milk, then the egg, into the flour. You might need to add a tablespoon of warm water to help it mix and work to a soft dough. Knead with the dough hook for 6-8 minutes until smooth and elastic, or turn out on to a lightly floured work surface and knead for about 10 minutes.

3 Put the dough in a lightly oiled bowl, cover with oiled cling film and leave to rise in a warm place for an hour or more, until doubled in size. Divide into 15 pieces and roll into balls. Place spaced apart in a traybake tin, cover with oiled cling film and allow to prove again for 15-30 minutes until well risen. Set the oven to Gas Mark 5 or 190°C.

4 To make the crosses: Mix the flour with the oil and blend in 5-6 tablespoons water until smooth. Put the mixture in a paper piping bag. Pipe crosses on the buns. Bake the buns for about 25 minutes.

5 To make the glaze: Heat sugar in a pan with 6 tablespoons cold water until it dissolves, then increase the heat and boil rapidly for 2 minutes to make a light syrup. Take buns out of oven and brush with sugar syrup. Serve warm.

※ To freeze: Cool on a wire rack, pack in a freezer box, seal and label. Use within 2 months. Thaw at room temperature, then warm through in the oven or microwave.

POST - CARD

Reader Barbara Pirie, from Henbury in Bristol, nominates the Poet's Walk in Clevedon, Somerset

'Just a short bus ride away from my home in Bristol is my favourite place – it's a coastal walk called Poet's Walk, in Clevedon. As a writer of poetry in my spare time, I can't fail to find inspiration amongst the gentle lapping of the waves and nature's best, as it is teeming with wildlife all year round.'

13 Monday

14 Tuesday

15 Wednesday

16 Thursday

17 Friday

18 Saturday

19 Sunday

Have A Go At... Tapestry

Use bright, modern colours to stitch this simple picture of a charming chick

This tapestry picture is worked on canvas using tapestry wool, which is similar to 4-ply knitting wool. Always use a tapestry needle as it has a large eye and a blunt point, making it easy to thread. Half-cross stitch – used here – is the most popular stitch to use on single-thread canvas.

You will need

- 16cm square of 12-count single-thread canvas
- Masking tape
- Size 18 tapestry needle
- 1 skein each of Appleton tapestry wool in the following colours: 434 mid- green, 432 light green, 943 candy pink, 855 mustard, 852 navy blue, 946 cerise, 753 dusky pink, and 704 peach
- Air-erasable fabric pen
- 9.8cm square of thick card
- Strong sewing thread and sewing needle
- 10cm picture frame

50 x 50cm square of 12-count interlock canvas; tapestry wool, all from a selection at Sew Exciting! (020 3068 0068; sewexciting.com)

Stitch diagram and key

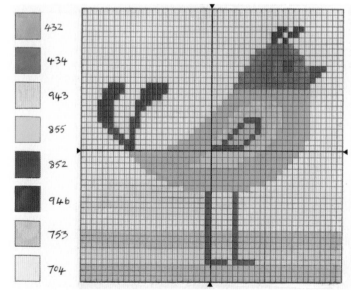

	432
	434
	943
	855
	852
	946
	753
	704

1 First, carefully stick some small pieces of masking tape over the four edges of the canvas to stop them from unravelling while you work. Measure the canvas using a ruler and find the approximate centre point. Next, use an air-erasable pen to draw a line along the horizontal and vertical threads that cross at the centre. The reason for doing this is that the drawn lines will help when you start to follow the chart – and then they will slowly fade away.

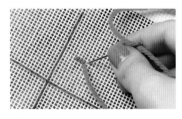

2 Thread a single length of wool through the tapestry needle. Refer to the chart to start stitching anywhere on the canvas, working left to right: bring the needle to the right side, leaving a 5cm trailing end of wool. To form a diagonal stitch, insert the needle one intersection of threads up and to the right. Bring the needle out one thread below. Repeat to stitch a row of diagonal stitches, stitching over the trailing end of thread on the underside.

3 Work next row from right to left, keeping the diagonal stitches in same direction as the previous row and so on, alternating the direction of the rows. All stitches will be vertical on the back of the canvas.

A tapestry frame will keep your work taut but isn't necessary on small items like this picture.

For many more great craft ideas and kits, including this striking kingfisher to cross-stitch, check out the Woman's Weekly Shop at womans weeklyshop.com

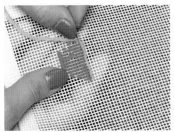

4 When you are close to running out of wool or need to change colour, insert needle through the back of about 5 stitches, pull the wool through and cut off the excess.

5 When you have finished, carefully peel off the tapes. Press under 1cm on the raw edges. Place the square of thick card centrally on the wrong side of the picture. Thread a 60cm-long double length of strong sewing thread on to a sewing needle. Fasten the thread to the centre on one pressed edge of the canvas. Sew the two opposite edges together with long interlacing stitches about 1.5cm apart. Pull the thread taut as you work. Fasten thread securely when you reach the edge of the card. Repeat to stitch from centre in the other direction. Sew the adjacent opposite edges together in the same way. Fix the tapestry in a picture frame.

Tapestry tips

❀ When buying Appleton tapestry wool, ask for the wool by code rather than colour, which is given only as a guide.
❀ Tapestry wool comes in skeins (about 10m) and hanks (about 40m). Don't cut the wool longer than 45cm, otherwise it may fray and tangle.
❀ With the needle threaded with a single length of wool, start with a long overlap and shorten it as you work to avoid the wool wearing close to the needle eye. If it tangles, let it dangle with the needle at the bottom – the needle's weight will unwind it.
❀ Canvas is available in mesh gauges measured by the number of holes to the inch; the higher the count, the smaller the holes.

MISSED Cues

All the couples she knew had an affinity with each other. They couldn't even turn up for a date on the same day

They always seemed to be missing each other. When Andy said they'd meet outside the Odeon at six somehow she ended up outside the Vue, or when she said they'd get together for drinks after work on Thursday he'd turn up on Wednesday.

'If we ever get married do you think we'll both turn up at the same church?' Andy joked.

'Or even on the same day?'

They chuckled over the idea before he backtracked and said: 'Not that I'm asking you, not yet, let's not assume...'

'God forbid!' she agreed, not wanting to appear needy.

All the couples they knew seemed to have an affinity with each other – some finished the other's sentences or knew what their partner was feeling. Lisa was beginning to wonder whether she and Andy were right for each other, even though she was crazy about him.

Maybe he was having similar thoughts, for the next time they went out, he said, 'Do you think we'll reach a point when our quirks will just annoy each other?'

'No doubt; it happens to everyone in time.'

'But when we can't even get times and places right; it's as if we're not listening to each other.'

'Then we have to make more of an effort,' Lisa urged, her heart beating a little faster – was this the moment when he called it off?

'My birthday's coming up, why don't you surprise me?' he said.

'Is this a test?'

'It could be.'

'Alright, then I want you to take me somewhere different next weekend, somewhere you think I'd really like.'

They both knew this would be a defining moment.

'Agreed.' He extended a business-like hand.

'Agreed,' she nodded and clasped his hand. Then they kissed; that worked if nothing else did.

What could she get Andy that would show how in tune with him she was? A computer game? An accessory for his bike? A sweater? All welcome, but nothing that screamed, 'I've really thought about this!'

Then she remembered how crestfallen he'd been a couple of weeks ago when she'd seen him signing a cheque with a cheap ballpoint pen.

'Where's your posh one?' she'd asked.

'It needs a refill. It's so old they don't make them any more. I loved that pen.'

First of all Lisa thought she could buy him a new one to replace it, until she decided that what he'd really appreciate would be his old one in working order again. She logged onto the internet to see if she could find a refill – surely there must be someone selling discontinued lines?

After hours of research she finally

Was this the moment he called it off?

located someone who could sell her a refill. It was expensive – it would have been cheaper to buy a new pen – but she knew it would be worth it to see Andy's face light up. Then he'd realise that they were meant for each other after all, that she could read his deepest needs.

Now, would he be able to do the same for her?

Andy picked her up at eleven on Saturday.

'Where are we going?' Lisa said in anticipation as she fastened her seatbelt. All sorts of things had been going through her mind – a spa day, lunch at a country hotel, a theatre matinee, surfing lessons; all would have been welcome.

'Wait and see,' he said secretively.

Her heart sank when half an hour later a fairground came in sight, with a big wheel dominating the steel-grey sky.

'It's only here for a few days.' Andy beamed. 'I haven't been to a proper fairground for years. How about you?'

'No,' she agreed. How could she tell him

that she'd never really liked the fair, not since that day she'd wanted to get off the waltzer but couldn't? Everyone ignored her screams, then she'd thrown up all over her best friend, and all the boys they'd been trying to impress had laughed at her. They'd never let her live it down in school.

She allowed him to lead her into the lights and noise and the smell of candyfloss and frying onions.

'What would you like to go on first?' He looked like an excited kid.

'You choose.' Lisa swallowed her fear. She didn't want to disappoint him. 'Not the waltzers though,' she quickly added; she couldn't face that.

She steeled herself as they rode the wheel, the bumper cars, the swings, the ghost train. She screamed, she cried, she shut her eyes, she bit her lip so hard that she drew blood. But she wasn't sick and after a while it didn't feel so bad.

'Why don't you want to try the waltzers?' Andy asked as they wandered past the swirling ride. She told him about her teenage experience. He didn't laugh or make her feel silly for avoiding them.

'Let's have a coffee,' she suggested. 'I can give you your birthday present.'

They sat in a greasy spoon. Lisa handed over the package. Andy looked intrigued as he began to fiddle with the wrapping while she held her breath. He was going to be so delighted! When he took out the refill he stared at it for a moment.

'I know how you love that pen,' Lisa filled the silence. 'It took me ages to track that down."

'Oh, Lisa.' He shook his head. 'I threw it away a week ago. I thought I'd never find a refill and it seemed pointless keeping it.'

She stared at him, open-mouthed. 'I hate fairs,' she retaliated.

Andy began to laugh.

'There's no hope for us,' he said.

But there was, she knew there was and she laughed, too, because they were both as hopeless as each other.

THE END

© Susan Sarapuk, 2013

20 Monday

21 Tuesday

22 Wednesday

23 Thursday

24 Friday

25 Saturday

26 Sunday

Making Your
Garden Grow

Got a few minutes (or an hour) to spare? Choose from Adrienne Wild's easy springtime jobs

If you only have...

5 Minutes

Set beer traps to protect the newly emerging shoots of herbaceous perennials, such as delphiniums, peonies, lupins, hostas, dicentra and aquilegia, from hungry slugs and snails.

10 Minutes

Plant calla lilies and cannas in large terracotta pots, ready to add an exotic touch to your summer patio.

Weed a little every day and it will be easier to keep your garden looking great.

15 Minutes

Sow seeds of tender vegetables such as chilli, aubergines, sweet peppers, tomatoes and cucumbers in trays on the windowsill, so you have good-sized plants to plant out in the garden for mid-May.

Erect a 60cm plastic or fleece screen around carrot rows to prevent carrot-root flies from laying eggs nearby.

Top-dress large plants that are growing in big pots by scraping away a few centimetres of old compost and replacing it with fresh.

30 Minutes

Trim to shape shrubs, such as buddlejas that flower in mid-to late-summer on current season's wood.

Prune winter-flowering *Clematis cirrhosa* to keep it in good shape. Once the blooms on flowering shoots have faded, cut back by a third.

Shred or chop up shrubby prunings and mix them with grass clippings before adding to the compost bin, and you'll have a ready supply of free mulch in the autumn.

Plant herbs in decorative pots, keeping them near the house for easy access.

20 Minutes

Save money by planting up summer baskets now with plugs or mini plants. Keep them in a warm, light spot indoors – by the time they can go outside, when the threat of frost has passed, your plants will be well established.

27 Monday

28 Tuesday

29 Wednesday

30 Thursday

1 Friday

2 Saturday

3 Sunday

MAY

4 Monday BANK HOLIDAY

5 Tuesday

6 Wednesday

7 Thursday

8 Friday

9 Saturday

10 Sunday

You will need

- 10mm square tiles: we used Quadra mini Nebula – approximately 56 Ottoman Treasure in New Green; 40 White Diamond, all from a selection at Mosaic Trader (01227 459350; mosaictraderuk.co.uk)
- 15mm square tiles: we used Italian Quadra tiles – approximately 30 Starlight foil-backed 'Scorpio'; 25 Opaline iridescent 'Asparagus'; Lucid clear 'Lawn Green'; all from a selection at Mosaic Trader (as before)
- Bowl – we used Farringdon mixing bowl 0.5ltr in stainless steel, from a selection at Colanders Cookshop (01438 314011; colanders cookshop.co.uk)
- Several pieces of thin china – saucers or side plates are ideal to use
- Wheeled nippers
- Safety goggles
- Silicone glue
- Craft syringe
- 1kg grout
- An old pot for mixing grout
- A small stick to mix grout – a lollipop stick or coffee stirrer, for example
- Disposable gloves
- Cloth/newspaper
- Craft knife or skewer

Bowled Over

Create a stunning, one-of-a-kind mosaic bowl with recycled china and pretty iridescent tiles

It may be a pain when you break a favourite bowl or plate, but why not save the pieces and use them to make something special, such as this beautiful bowl. You can either use an old ceramic or metal bowl as the base. If you use metallic, the shiny metal surface gleams appealingly through the iridescent tiles. We have given specific instructions for the 0.5 litre bowl listed right – adapt for a smaller or larger bowl accordingly, ensuring you plan out your design before you get started.

1 For the floral-printed tiles, you will need to cut 11 circles of china each measuring approximately 20mm in diameter. Select china with suitable motifs, including one feature piece for the centre. If you

don't have a piece of broken china you'd like to use, find cheap pieces in charity shops and at car boot sales. Select the patterned areas required and roughly cut around them, wearing goggles – place the jaws of the tile nippers over the edge of the china and squeeze; repeat several times, trying to save the important areas of the plate.

2 Cut out the designs roughly and then nibble very closely and precisely using tiny 'nips' around the selected motifs. It's not essential to achieve a perfectly round shape; an approximate circle is fine. It's a good idea to work within a box to stop the pieces shooting away too far.

3 When you have 11, 20mm circles of china, place your centre piece in the middle of the bowl, arrange 10 x 10mm square green Ottoman Treasure tiles around it, then the ten remaining circles. Using a syringe to apply silicone glue to the bowl, stick the central piece of china into the base of the bowl, then the circle of green squares, followed by your cut circles. This part of the design should measure approximately 80mm across and should finish just as the sides of the bowl start to curve upwards. Do not use so much adhesive that it squeezes up between tiles, as it will later show as peaks when the bowl is grouted. If there is excess glue, it can be removed when it has set using a sharp craft knife or skewer.

4 Apply a line of glue all the way around the top of the bowl where it becomes flat. Putting the adhesive into a craft syringe makes it very easy to be precise about the quantity of glue being laid, especially on fiddly areas like this. Press the green mini Ottoman Treasure tiles into the adhesive, close together but not touching, all the way around the top of the bowl. Try not to apply too much glue.

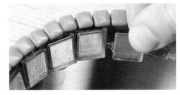

5 Select the foil-backed metallic Quadra Starlight tiles and lay them onto another line of adhesive under the rim, aligning with the top of the bowl. Gravity may pull the tiles down slightly, so keep an eye on them and reposition as necessary. Stick the next row of 10mm square Mini Nebula white tiles in place, followed by the row of mint-coloured Iridescent Opaline tiles. Keep checking the positioning of the rows, ensuring they are even and they do not slip.

6 The Lucid clear 'Lawn Green' tiles are used to create the final row. To accommodate the curve of the bowl, every other one of the tiles in this last row must be a half tile. To nip into two equal pieces, place the nippers over the centre of the tile and squeeze. Hold onto the pieces as you do so, or they may disappear across the table.

7 Lay these clear tiles very carefully as they are totally transparent. It is essential that the entire back of each tile is completely coated in adhesive as any gaps will allow the grout to run behind the tiles and show from the front. Lay the tiles one by one and use plenty of adhesive, dispensing glue from the syringe helps with the accuracy required.

8 Leave the bowl aside for 24 hours for the adhesive to set. Before grouting, check there is no excess adhesive rising up between or on top of the tiles. If there is, it can be removed using a craft knife or skewer. Mix the grout to a toothpaste-like consistency wearing gloves and a mask. Use your gloved hands to place it into the bowl and push it into all the crevices, taking special care to make a neat edge around the top row. Clear as much grout away as possible using the side of your thumb, taking care around the sharp edges of the china.

9 Leave to dry for 10 minutes or so and then clear away the remainder of the grout using scrunched-up newspaper. If it is not coming away easily, leave for a few more minutes and try again. Sprinkling a little dry grout powder can help dry up the surface if the grout is a bit wet. Put aside until the grout is completely dry and polish with a ball of scrunched-up newspaper or a soft cloth.

Mosaic: Anne Cardwell (makingmosaics.co.uk). Photos: Lunette Chapman. Styling: Dilly Orme

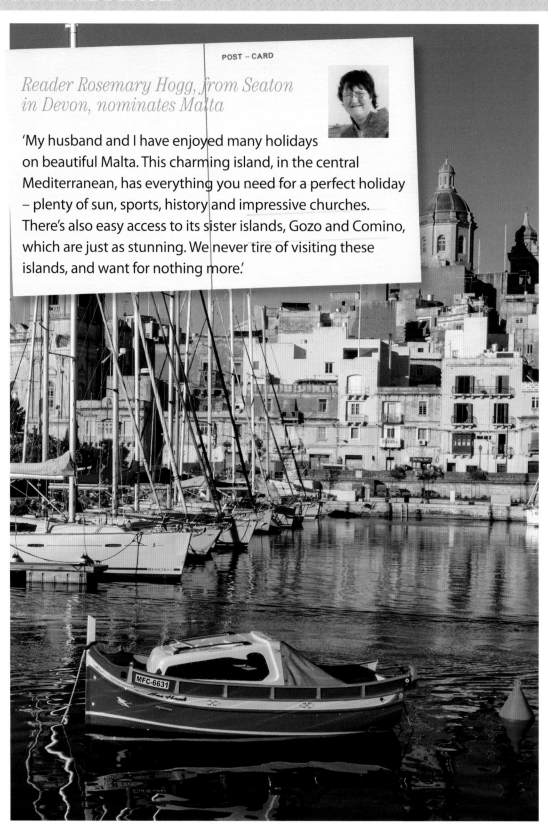

POST – CARD

Reader Rosemary Hogg, from Seaton in Devon, nominates Malta

'My husband and I have enjoyed many holidays on beautiful Malta. This charming island, in the central Mediterranean, has everything you need for a perfect holiday – plenty of sun, sports, history and impressive churches. There's also easy access to its sister islands, Gozo and Comino, which are just as stunning. We never tire of visiting these islands, and want for nothing more.'

11 Monday

12 Tuesday

13 Wednesday

14 Thursday

15 Friday

16 Saturday

17 Sunday

Floral Placemat

Prettify your tea table with our crochet design, made up of motifs worked in trebles and chain

- Easy-peasy
- A Bit More Tricky
- **Hard-ish**
- Quite A Challenge

MEASUREMENTS
48cm/19in by 32cm/12½in.

MATERIALS
1 x 100g ball of DMC Petra 3 (100% cotton) in Primrose (5745). Size 2.50 crochet hook. You can buy the yarn online at womansweeklyshop.com/yarn or call 0800 024 1212.

TENSION
Each motif measures 16cm in diameter, using 2.50 hook.

ABBREVIATIONS
Ch, chain; **dc**, double crochet; **st**, stitch; **tr**, treble; **trtr**, triple treble; **slst**, slip stitch; **chsp**, chain space.

NOTE
Yarn amounts are based on average requirements and are approximate. Instructions in square brackets are worked as stated after 2nd bracket.

TOP ROW

Left motif
With size 2.50 hook make 9ch, slst in first ch to form a ring.
1st round: 3ch (counts as 1tr), 23tr in ring, slst in 3rd of 3ch – 24 sts.
2nd round: 3ch (counts as 1tr), miss st at base of 3ch, 1tr in next tr, 3ch, miss next tr, [1tr in each of next 2tr, 3ch, miss next tr] 7 times, slst in 3rd of 3ch. **3rd round:** 3ch (counts as 1tr), miss st at base of 3ch, 2tr in next tr, 4ch, [1tr in next tr, 2tr in next tr, 4ch] 7 times, slst in 3rd of 3ch.
4th round: 3ch (counts as 1tr), miss st at base of 3ch, 2tr in next tr, 1tr in next tr, 5ch, [1tr in next tr, 2tr in next tr, 1tr in next tr, 5ch] 7 times, slst in 3rd of 3ch. **5th round:** 3ch (counts as 1tr), miss st at base of 3ch, 2tr in each of next 3tr, 3ch, [1tr in next tr, 2tr in each of next 3tr, 3ch] 7 times, slst in 3rd of 3ch. **6th round:** 3ch (counts as 1tr), miss st at base of 3ch, 1tr in each of next 2tr, work 1tr, 2ch and 1tr in next tr, 1tr in each of next 3tr, 2ch, [1tr in each of next 3tr, work 1tr, 2ch and 1tr in next tr, 1tr in each of next 3tr, 2ch] 7 times, slst in

3rd of 3ch. **7th round:** Slst in each st to first chsp, slst in chsp, 6ch (counts as 1trtr and 1ch), [1trtr, 1ch] 9 times in same chsp as last slst, 1dc in next chsp, 1ch, * [1trtr, 1ch] 10 times in next chsp, 1dc in next chsp, 1ch, repeat from * 6 times more, slst in 5th of 6ch. **8th round:** Slst in first chsp, 1ch (does not count as a st), 1dc in same chsp, [work 1dc, 3ch and 1dc in each of next 7 chsp, 1dc in each of next 4 chsp] 7 times, work 1dc, 3ch and 1dc in each of next 7 chsp, 1dc in each of last 3 chsp, slst in first dc – 8 scallops. Fasten off.

Centre motif
Work as left motif to end of 7th round.
8th round: Slst in first chsp, 1ch (does not count as a st), 1dc in same chsp, [work 1dc, 3ch and 1dc in each of next 7 chsp, 1dc in each of next 4 chsp] 6 times, work 1dc, 3ch and 1dc in each of next 3 chsp, 1dc in next chsp, 1ch, miss first 3 chsp on any scallop of left motif, slst in next chsp on left motif, 1ch, 1dc in same chsp as last dc, [1dc in next chsp, 1ch, slst in next chsp of left motif, 1ch, 1dc in same chsp as last dc] twice, work 1dc, 3ch and 1dc in next chsp, 1dc in each of next 4 chsp, work 1dc, 3ch and 1dc in next chsp, 1dc in next chsp, 1ch, miss first chsp on next scallop of left motif, slst in next chsp of left motif, 1ch, 1dc in same chsp as last dc, [1dc in next chsp, 1ch, slst in next chsp of left motif, 1ch, 1dc in same chsp as last dc] twice, work 1dc, 3ch and 1dc in each of next 3 chsp, 1dc in each of last 3 chsp, slst in first dc. Fasten off.

Right motif
Work as centre motif but on 8th round join to middle 2 of the remaining 6 scallops of centre motif.

BOTTOM ROW

Left motif
Work as centre motif on top row, but on 8th round join to lower 2 scallops of left motif on top row.

Centre motif
Work as left motif on top row to end of 7th round.

8th round: Slst in first chsp, 1ch (does not count as a st), 1dc in same chsp, [work 1dc, 3ch and 1dc in each of next 7 chsp, 1dc in each of next 4 chsp] 4 times, ** work 1dc, 3ch and 1dc in each of next 3 chsp, 1dc in next chsp, 1ch, miss first 3 chsp on first of lower 2 scallops of centre motif on top row, slst in next chsp of centre motif on top row, 1ch, 1dc in same chsp as last dc, [1dc in next chsp, 1ch, slst in next chsp of centre motif on top row, 1ch, 1dc in same chsp as last dc] twice, work 1dc, 3ch and 1dc in next chsp, 1dc in each of next 4 chsp, work 1dc, 3ch and 1dc in next chsp, 1dc in next chsp, 1ch, miss first chsp on next scallop of centre motif on top row, slst in next chsp of centre motif on top row, 1ch, 1dc in same chsp as last dc, [1dc in next chsp, 1ch, slst in next chsp of centre motif on top row, 1ch, 1dc in same chsp as last dc] twice, work 1dc, 3ch and 1dc in each of next 3 chsp **, 1dc in each of next 4 chsp, repeat from ** to ** but join to next 2 scallops of left motif on bottom row, 1dc in each of last 3 chsp, slst in first dc. Fasten off.

Right motif
Work as centre motif of bottom row but join to lower 2 scallops of right motif on top row, then to next 2 scallops of centre motif on bottom row.

Filler motif (make 2)
With size 2.50 hook make 9ch, slst in first ch to form a ring.
1st round: 3ch (counts as 1tr), 23tr in ring, slst in 3rd of 3ch – 24 sts.
2nd round: 1ch (does not count as a st), 1dc in same place as slst, 6ch, slst in centre chsp of the 3 chsp on any scallop in gap where 4 motifs meet, 6ch, [1dc in each of next 3 sts of 1st round, 6ch, slst in centre chsp of the 3 chsp on next scallop in gap where 4 motifs meet, 6ch] 7 times, 1dc in each of last 2 sts, slst in first dc. Fasten off.

TO MAKE UP
Pin out to correct measurements and press as given on ball band.

Your Good Health

Ask Dr Mel

Q I've been suffering with a niggly cough for some time now. How should I put up with my cough before going to see my GP about it?

A Coughs that drag on are surprisingly common. US researchers recently found that acute cough illnesses can last on average 18 days, although patients expected their coughs to settle in half that time.

If you're basically healthy and develop a cough, with or without coloured phlegm, you won't usually benefit from antibiotics. But you may want to dose yourself with pharmacy remedies, such as paracetamol (for fever or sore throat), decongestant lozenges, a vapour rub and/or cough medicine to soothe an irritating night-time cough. It's important to drink extra fluids, and I'd suggest inhaling steam from a bowl of hot water, too.

As a GP, cough duration usually worries me less than linked symptoms, recent foreign travel, and co-existing conditions such as lung/heart disease or diabetes. Seek medical advice promptly if you also have breathlessness, wheezing, chest pain, extreme weakness, blood-stained phlegm, high fever or confusion, as these can be signs of pneumonia and other serious conditions. And, as a lingering cough is occasionally a sign of cancer, TB, or other diseases, national guidelines say you'll need a chest X-ray if it lasts more than three weeks.

TAKE 5...
Ways To Beat Fungal Infections

1 LET THE AIR circulate – wear loose clothing in natural fibres and bathe/shower daily.

2 KEEP NAIL CUTICLES healthy – don't pick or nibble!

3 AVOID prolonged, moist conditions; wear cotton lining gloves inside rubber gloves, and dry hands, feet and nails carefully.

4 AVOID SWEATY FEET – change your socks daily, take off your trainers as soon as you get home.

5 RINSE your mouth after using an inhaled steroid or try using a 'spacer' device instead.

A Great Exercise To...
Strengthen your core

The Plank

Crouch down on to your elbows and knees, hands clasped in front of you. Straighten your legs, feet hip-width apart, and go on to the balls of your feet. Face the floor and keep a straight line – don't arch your back or stick your bottom in the air. Pull your tummy in and breathe easily. Hold for 20 seconds and increase to a minute as you get stronger. *Well done!*

TIP
Once you can hold a basic plank, try lifting one leg straight off the ground. Hold for two seconds and swap legs. Keep your alignment and don't twist.

HOW THE EXPERTS STAY HEALTHY
Marcelle Pick, nurse and author

What's in your medicine cabinet?
Vitamin C – I always take it when I think I'm coming down with a cold; and Airborne, to help boost my immune system.

What's good in your fridge?
Millet-and-flax roll-ups; they're gluten free and can be filled with anything – great for a quick snack or lunch. I always have blueberries and raspberries at the ready, too.

What's your favourite exercise?
Aerobics three or four times a week.

What's a real foodie treat?
Greek yogurt with berries and a little Stevia (a natural sweetener).

What makes you happy?
Making jewellery and sewing. Biking is one of my favourite outdoor activities, and I absolutely love ballroom dancing.

What's the secret of a good night's sleep?
Reminding myself that worrying about things doesn't change the outcome, and doing something relaxing an hour or so before I settle down to sleep.

● *Is It Me Or My Hormones?* (Hay House, £12.99) by Marcelle Pick, founder of the Women To Women clinic (womentowomen.com), is out now.

18 Monday

19 Tuesday

20 Wednesday

21 Thursday

22 Friday

23 Saturday

24 Sunday

New Potato & Ham Hash

Serves 3-4	
Calories: 380	
Fat: 20g	
Saturated fat: 12g	
Suitable for freezing: ✗	

* 60g (2oz) butter
* 1 small onion, peeled, cut into wedges, leaves pulled apart
* 750g (1½lb) new potatoes, scrubbed, cooked until just tender, then thickly sliced
* 200g (7oz) thick piece of cooked ham (from the deli counter)
* Salt and freshly ground black pepper
* Freshly grated nutmeg and paprika pepper
* 2-3 tablespoons chopped fresh parsley
* 4 plum tomatoes, quartered and de-seeded
* 60g (2oz) Cheddar, grated

1 Heat half the butter in a large pan over a medium heat. Add onion and fry until tender.

2 Add the rest of the butter and, when melted, tip in the slices of potato. Let them brown in the pan for about 5 minutes.

3 Cut the ham into 1cm (½in) chunks and add to the pan. Season with a little salt and lots of black pepper, some nutmeg and paprika. Add half the parsley. Stir well, press the mixture down in the pan, and leave to cook over a medium heat for about 8 minutes until browned underneath.

4 Stir the mixture, scraping up the bits from the bottom of the pan, press it down again and leave for another 5-8 minutes to brown again.

5 Stir in the tomatoes, and sprinkle with grated cheese. Put the lid on the pan and leave on a low heat for about 5 minutes for the cheese to melt. Serve hot, sprinkled with the rest of the parsley.

Note: You can use any left-over cooked meat in this dish.

The Numbers Game

When George and I planned our retirement, puzzles were never mentioned

'Well, that wasn't bad, even if I do say so myself,' he says as he put down his pen and the book of Sudoku puzzles with a satisfied grunt. 'That only took me 18 minutes. The guide time says 25.'

'That's very good, well done,' I reply, trying to inject some enthusiasm into my voice. Truth to tell I am bored with George's current obsession with Sudoku. I mean, what is the satisfaction in writing the numbers one to nine, in a grid nine by nine, in nine different variations?

'Do you fancy coming to help me in the garden?' I say to try and distract him. 'I could do with your help to tie up that cotoneaster against the back fence.'

'OK' he replies. 'You go ahead. I'll just make a start on this next puzzle until you're ready for me.'

And that's it; he's got his head down, his brow furrowed in concentration as he pores over the book again, mouthing the mantra of numbers, occasionally stopping while he writes another answer on the grid. I am so frustrated. When we'd planned our retirement, number puzzles were never mentioned. Or perhaps they were and I simply misheard and instead imagined all those plans about days out, pottering around the garden together and spending more time away at the caravan? I smile at my own sorry joke, then realise how sad and lonely that makes me feel before deciding to get on with my jobs.

Sighing deeply I change into my clogs and pull on the old jacket and gloves that I keep for outside work. It's a beautiful day and perfect weather for gardening: the sun is shining for what feels like the first time in weeks, and there's a coolness in there air that's refreshing. I walk around the perimeter to assess the damage the recent winds have caused. It's not just the cotoneaster that needs some extra support, I think as I make a mental note to add some more stakes to the dahlias and the gladioli. I take the hedging shears and attack the hedge the previous next-door neighbour had insisted on planting too close to our fence: it overhangs and has been a constant battle to keep under control. After 30 minutes of furious hacking I step back over the mound of fallen branches and realise that the once lush evergreen trees are looking threadbare. Perhaps taking my frustrations out on the hedge wasn't a good idea. I pop next door to apologise and take a pot of marmalade with me as a peace offering.

Marg greets me with a smile and the ever-welcome cup of tea. It's only three months since she moved in, but it feels as though we've been friends for ever. She laughs about the hedge and reassures me that she had thought it too big for the garden, then asks if I'd mind if she had it removed. Which, of course, I don't. So that's one problem resolved.

Marg laughs even more when I explain how it is that I came to be wielding the hedging shears with such unrestrained

I smile at my own sorry joke

violence. Soon we're helpless with laughter as we recount tales of trivial frustrations and the silly things we have done. I tell her about the time that I turned the batteries around inside the TV remote to stop George flicking aimlessly through the channels when I wanted to watch my favourite soap; Marg tells me about the time that she upended a bowl of trifle on her first husband's head after a tiff; about the time she threw her second husband's golf clubs in the skip; about the time she put pink hair dye in the shampoo bottle just before her husband (her first or third? I've lost count) went out to a sportsman's dinner...

And as she carries on with her stories of past marital disharmony, something registers in my brain. George and I may not enjoy the most exciting life but we are happy together. Sudoku is such a trivial thing for me to be getting myself worked up over. What I need to do is remind George of all the things we planned to do now we're free of work commitments. I don't want to complain but I do want to get my point across to him in a gentle way.

Back at home I make lunch. I open a tin of anchovies and lay them out to make a grid across the pizza before I pop it in the oven. Setting out the accompanying salad on a large tray, I carefully arrange precisely nine of each of the salad bits and pieces: cherry tomatoes, radishes, cucumber slices, baby beetroots, pickled onions, slices of red pepper, celery chunks, slices of egg, lumps of cheese. Then I prepare nine envelopes on which I write the numbers one to nine before I call George in.

'Is it that time already?' he says innocently as he joins me in the kitchen. 'I thought you were going to give me a shout when you needed me in the garden.'

As he sits at the table he looks bemused at the numerically precise presentation of lunch. I raise my eyebrows and give him a smile, challenging him to work it out. He examines the food quizzically and I see his expression change slowly from confusion to awareness through to embarrassment, before he finally smiles back at me.

'Sorry,' he says sheepishly. 'I have been rather engrossed in my puzzles, haven't I?'

'Just a bit,' I reply, trying but failing to keep the irony out of my voice. I soften my answer with a giggle which he returns before we both laugh.

'I don't mind, really I don't,' I reassure him. 'But it would be nice to do some things together as well. So I thought we could both play a numbers game.'

I offer him the nine envelopes and ask him to choose a number between one and nine. Taking one he opens it and reads what I have written inside: *Go for a walk along the beach*. Which is what we do after lunch. He likes this game and we agree to open another envelope tomorrow at breakfast to fix our plan for the day.

Before I go to bed that night I take a pen and write out nine new cards to put into the envelopes, one of which we will open at breakfast. Each card reads: *Potter in the garden*. I smile to myself. It's only a little deception, after all.

THE END

© Beatrice Charles, 2013

25 Monday SPRING BANK HOLIDAY

26 Tuesday

27 Wednesday

28 Thursday

29 Friday

30 Saturday

31 Sunday

PUZZLES

Pathfinder

Beginning after the highlighted letter E, you must follow a continuous path through the letters to find a vegetable listed below. The trail passes through each and every letter once, and may twist up, down or sideways but never diagonally.

ASPARAGUS   ENDIVE
AUBERGINE   LEEK
BROCCOLI   PARSNIP
CABBAGE   POTATO
CARROT   SPINACH
CAULIFLOWER   SWEDE
COURGETTE   TURNIP

D	N	E	A	S	P	A	R	A	G
I	V	E	H	C	A	N	R	B	U
L	F	L	E	E	K	I	O	E	S
O	I	L	U	A	S	P	C	D	A
W	T	T	E	C	L	O	C	E	U
E	E	G	R	U	I	T	S	W	B
R	R	N	I	O	C	O	B	A	E
T	U	P	P	A	R	R	B	C	R
S	R	A	O	C	O	P	A	E	G
N	I	P	T	A	T	E	G	N	I

Linkwords

Fit 10 words into the grid so that each links with the end of the word on its left and the beginning of the one on the right. Then unscramble the letters in the shaded squares to make a word. Clue: *An English county (9).*

You can work it out...

CREAM — TRIFLE
PASSION — POWER
BRANDY — BEAN
BOMBER — POTATO
CLOSE — TICKET
DAWN — LINE
ROYAL — TREE
HERBACEOUS — COLLIE
VICTORIA — BAG

Solutions to this month's puzzles on August puzzles

SOLUTIONS FOR MARCH 2015

JUNE

Quandries, Crises & Tips

It's the biggest day of a woman's life, but with so many choices and potential faux pas to make, brides needed someone to turn to for reliable practical, emotional and fashion advice

Auntie Gertie told me my trousseau would cost from three to seven hundred pounds

WOMAN'S WEEKLY

Do Men Marry for Looks?

The Belief that Men Don't Want Intelligent Wives Refuses to be Killed, and Men Wouldn't Dream of Telling

him. That's satisfactory, *so far as it goes*, but, if you happen to be at all observant, you will, no doubt, have noticed that, as a rule, it doesn't stretch as far as the altar steps. That is, unless the pretty face carries something behind it.

The standard of marriage has risen—that's why single blessedness is so much on the increase. We want the *best* and *highest* in marriage; we refuse to have a poor substitute. We are going *forward*, not backward, as some people would have us believe. And men are not behind in the desire to get the best out of marriage. The average man knows that it takes a great deal more than a pretty face to make a happy, successful marriage. And so the mere beauty is not chosen for a life-long companion, however agreeably she may have filled up a gap before marriage.

The belief that men don't want intelligent women as wives refuses to be killed off, and then themselves wouldn't dream of telling their friends and relations they intended marrying an intelligent woman. They've found a new name—they say she's "sensible," which isn't a bit the same, and they know it, but it sounds less alarming.

It's the woman with heart and brain

WE had a heated discussion the other evening as to whether men marry pretty faces. It was at the club, and we were divided into two camps, one declaring emphatically that men are intensely silly when a pretty face is concerned, never troubling to find out if there is anything behind it. The other camp hotly denied the soft impeachment, saying how often when we've been introduced to our friends' wives we've said afterwards : " Well, he can't have married her for her *looks*, because she hasn't got any." A man is certainly attracted by a pretty face. So are we, for that matter. And he

Decisions, decisions You could fret over every detail… or follow our tips. We made it sound so easy!

The love isle 'The music of breaking waves, birdsong and summer roses.' The South Coast was an ideal honeymoon spot

APRIL 11, 1936   251

HONEYMOON LAND !

Barbara Mole Will Help You With Your Holiday Problems. Write to her c/o "Woman's Weekly," The Fleetway House, Farringdon Street, London, E.C.4, enclosing a stamped, self-addressed envelope for a personal reply

THE time, the place and the loved one all together.

How often, when travelling, has that phrase haunted my mind! I find a little loneliness, tucked away in folds, secure and homely. The evening quiet but for the lowing of the cows coming home from the milking. A dream upbubbling through a tree-hung valley on its way to the seashore. The music of breaking waves on the pebbly beach. Bird song, and the scent of summer roses.

Surely this is the ideal spot for a honeymoon.

By now, perhaps you have guessed the secret. I am hunting out places for those of you who write : When is the perfect spot for us to go to for that most perfect honeymoon?

THE WILDS OF DORSET

THERE is a delightful, unspoilt coastline in Dorset. The grassy downs and fields end abruptly at the sea cliffs. It is a countryside of tiny beaches, fine which little streams make a track to the rocks where one can spend hours of perfect solitude with nothing but the sound of the sea, the screaming of the gulls, and the plaintive call of the darting peewits.

SOUTH DEVON

ON to Devon, to Lyme Regis, Budleigh Salterton and Beer.

The white cliffs turn red, and

A dream of a dress

A wedding gown can cost well into four figures, so hiring an outfit could be a more affordable option. The Cancer Research Campaign charity has now opened a special occasions hire shop, where more than 100 wedding dresses can be hired from £40 a week. The stock has been built up from dresses donated to the 170 CRC shops and includes new garments from manufacturers. Bridesmaids' dresses can also be hired from £20 and page-boy outfits from £15. CRC operates this service from its shop in Uckfield, East Sussex, where manager Janet Ormwood says, "Customers often

the sea a deeper blue. The tiny fishing ports are gay and picturesque. Devon lanes are high hedged with wild rose and honeysuckle, and the farmhouses are tucked snugly in their lush green fields. Honeymoon places, every one.

Now we come to Torquay, that sparkling, glittering resort. Palm trees and a riot of sub-tropical flowers grow here. The wide sweep of Tor Bay, the sunshine on the white hotels that look like palaces, make it as nearly a town as any on the Eastern Riviera. The choice for those who prefer a gay resort. Hotels and promenades to flaunt one's trousseau finery. Known to its genius to one's new evening's frocks. Laughter, lights and merriment as a background to the perfection of the occasion.

Near by Torquay is Babbacombe, quaint and severely rural, with gardens leading to the steep, red cliffs of the famous Oyce. This is the perfect combination of rural and complete

EXMOOR

THEN you come to the fascinating valley of the River Lyn. Steepwooded hills leave the rough moorland, and from the narrow gorge of this tumultuous, sparkling little waterfall of a river. This country is charged with romance. Those of you who have read "Lorna Doone" know that it is a fit setting for one of the greatest love stories.

So on, up past Woody Bay and the famous valley of the Rocks, over the moors again with the sea always booming against the rocks, till you come to quaint Combe Martin nestling by its tiny bay. (So again to [...]

LESSONS for SWEETHEARTS—

" *Tell Them That Petting Will Bring a Lot of Men Round You, But, Of Itself, It Will Never Get You A Good Husband,*" Said the American Girl.

Tell Them Never to Make Their Boy-Friend Think He Is All The World to Them.

worstish; what she didn't know about marriage wasn't worth knowing.

She had that they idea was that a woman should take as much trouble to get the necessary knowledge in feeling and choosing a husband as a farmer does in buying a horse.

"The days," she said, smiling, " of my in the romantic poke are over!"

THE MIDDLE WAY

I ADMIT to you that this shocked me a little. I never—well, while I was listening to her, I imagined myself falling in love with her. Which was not a good state in the imagination, for she was a good-looking and quite charming woman.

But I felt that it would be more difficult to fall in love with her if I knew that all the time, with all those letters in her head and probably of her large-scale, she was sizing me up and telling stock of me as a farmer who was buying a horse ! It seemed to take the joy of the glamour out of it.

And I felt that what would have to be taken continually hard or verily—

Gladys Fairclough, the film star, thinks it is most important for brides to learn how to entertain.

Romance or realism? A debate in 1938 (above) asked if a woman should 'take as much trouble finding a husband as a farmer does in buying a horse' – or whether that kills the romance

1 Monday

2 Tuesday

3 Wednesday

4 Thursday

5 Friday

6 Saturday

7 Sunday

Rosé Wine & Red Berry Jellies

Serves 6
Calories: 88
Fat: 0g
Saturated fat: 0g
Suitable for freezing: ✗

1 Bring about half the wine to a simmer in a small pan. Take off the heat, sprinkle in the sugar and whisk in the gelatine, a sheet at a time, until it dissolves.

2 Pour into a large jug, and stir in the rest of the wine and elderflower cordial, if using. Cool.

3 Pack the fruit into 6 glasses and pour in the cooled, almost-setting wine mixture. Chill for 2 hours, or until set.

* 350ml (12fl oz) rosé wine
* 2 tablespoons caster sugar
* 5 leaves gelatine
* 1 tablespoon elderflower cordial, optional
* About 600g (1¼lb) fruit: 250g (8oz) each strawberries and raspberries and 125g (4oz) blueberries

Tip from our kitchen

If the gelatine doesn't dissolve, just put the pan back on a low heat until it does.

POST – CARD

Reader Beverley Dodd, from Peasedown St John, Somerset, nominates Shanklin on the Isle of Wight

'My favourite place is Shanklin, Isle of Wight, because of its association with John Keats – he stayed and wrote there in 1819. Longfellow also stayed in the town, at the Crab Inn, and left a poem about it on a stone outside. The Crab was a coaching inn and now serves delicious food. Sandown Pier is fun, too!'

8 Monday

9 Tuesday

10 Wednesday

11 Thursday

12 Friday

13 Saturday

14 Sunday

So Then... And
Yet So Now

A gorgeous pattern taken from the WW archives (December 1956 to be precise), this delicate, ultra-feminine top hasn't dated one bit

MEASUREMENTS

To fit sizes 81 (86) (91) (97-102) cm/32 (34) (36) (38-40) in.
Actual measurements 83 (91) (99) (107) cm/32½ (36) (39) (42) in.
Side seam 30 (31) (32) (33) cm/ 11¾ (12¼) (12½) (13) in.
Length to shoulder 43 (45) (47) (49) cm/17 (17¾) (18½) (19¼) in.
Sleeve seams All sizes 10cm/4in.

MATERIALS

2 (3) (3) (3) 25g balls of Rico Design Fashion Romance in Grey (005). Pair of 3mm (No. 11) and 4mm (No. 8) knitting needles. You can buy the yarn online at womansweeklyshop.com/yarn or call 0800 024 1212.

TENSION

20 stitches and 34 rows, to 10 x 10cm, over lacy diamond pattern, using 4mm needles.

ABBREVIATIONS

K, knit; **p**, purl; **st**, stitch; **sl**, slip; **tog**, together; **psso**, pass slip st over; **skpo**, (sl1, k1, psso); **yf**, yarn forward to make a st.

NOTE

Yarn amounts are based on average requirements and are therefore approximate. Instructions are given for small size. Where they vary, work figures in round brackets for larger sizes. Instructions in square brackets are worked as stated after 2nd bracket.

BACK & FRONT

(both alike)
With 3mm needles, cast on 83 (91) (99) (107) sts.
1st rib row: K1, [p1, k1] to end.
2nd rib row: P1, [k1, p1] to end.
Repeat the last 2 rows until rib measures 12cm, ending with the 2nd row.
Change to 4mm needles.
1st row: K4, [yf, sl1, k2tog, psso, yf, k5] to last 7 sts, yf, sl1, k2tog, psso, yf, k4.
2nd row: K1, p to last st, k1.
3rd row: K2, [k2tog, yf, k3, yf, skpo, k1] to last 9 sts, k2tog, yf, k3, yf, skpo, k2.
4th row: K1, p to last st, k1.
5th row: K1, k2tog, yf, k5, [yf, sl1, k2tog, psso, yf, k5] to last 3 sts, yf, skpo, k1.
6th row: K1, p to last st, k1.
7th row: K3, [yf, skpo, k1, k2tog, yf, k3] to end.
8th row: K1, p to last st, k1.
These 8 rows form the pattern. Continue in pattern until work measures 30 (31) (32) (33) cm from beginning, ending with a right-side row.
Shape for sleeves: Cast on 16 sts, k1, p 15 across these 16 sts, p to end, turn and cast on 16 sts – 115 (123) (131) (139) sts.
Continue in pattern until work measures 40 (42) (44) (46) cm from beginning, ending with a wrong-side row.

NECK RIBBING

1st row: Pattern 35, p1, [k1, p1] 22 (26) (30) (34) times, pattern 35.
2nd row: K1, p33, k2, [p1, k1] 21 (25) (29) (33) times, p1, k2, p33, k1.
Working centre sts in rib as set, continue in pattern until work measures 43 (45) (47) (49) cm from beginning, ending with a wrong-side row.
Shape shoulders: Continue working as before and cast off 8 sts at beginning of next 8 rows and 3 sts at beginning of following 2 rows – 45 (53) (61) (69) sts.
Cast off loosely in rib.

SLEEVE EDGINGS

(both alike)
Leaving ribbed section free for neck opening, join shoulder seams. With right side facing and using 3mm needles, pick up and k89 (95) (101) (107) sts evenly along row-ends of sleeve.
1st rib row: P1, [k1, p1] to end.
2nd rib row: K1, [p1, k1] to end.
Repeat these 2 rows, once more, then work the 1st row again. Cast off loosely in rib.

TO MAKE UP

Join side and sleeve seams, including sleeve edgings.

Easy-peasy

A Bit More
Tricky

Hard-ish

**Quite A
Challenge**

Tea & Cake

He's as solid as fruit cake – or he was, until the
Eton Mess lady came into his life...

I see her as soon as I come in the main entrance. She is sitting at a table in the far left hand corner of the hall; she is easy to spot because she's half the age of every other stallholder. She is much as I expected: a bedhead blonde with pale skin, a strawberry red pout, and a fair bit of cleavage on show – the kind of woman who is irresistible to other women's husbands. But then maybe I am a tad prejudiced.

I collect my pot of tea and a slice of Madeira from the WI stall and sit at a table in the café section where I can watch her, unobserved. There are lots of people milling about. I don't think she will feel my gaze. I am not so interesting, and I won't stare. Even though my heart is beating so fast it's hard to act casual.

A gap opens up in the crowd and just for a second our eyes meet. Then an old lady carrying a shopping bag crosses the space, blocking her out. She doesn't look my way again. I'm not the kind of woman who warrants a second glance.

I am ordinary. Although Jack says I'm not. He says I'm soothing. 'Being with you is like eating apple pie and custard,' he says.

The blonde, the husband-stealer, is more Eton Mess.

I wipe cake crumbs from my mouth with a paper serviette. Will I have the courage to carry out my plan? I have to do it – not just for me. I think of Beth, a late but much wanted addition to our family, trundling round the kitchen on her pink balance bike.

'I doing it – look. I riding.'

I'm doing it too, I think, I'm riding on a very thin line – and this could go either way. What if I make things worse? I feel a bit sick.

This was a mad idea. Perhaps I should just leave. I can't though. Beth is only two. She needs both her parents. I don't want her to grow up in a fractured family, being passed between her mum and dad for weekend visits. I want her to know only security and love, as I did when I was a child.

I wait until the crowds begin to thin out a little, and some of the stallholders start to pack up their wares: jewellery, bric-a-brac, home-made cards. I used to love these sales when I was a teenager, wandering around the other stalls while my father sat behind his usual table, selling old postcards of Dorset. You never knew what you were going to find. Once I found a vintage Versace bag for 50p. I was the envy of my friends for weeks.

I take a deep breath, then I get up and go across to her stall. She is selling kids stuff: Lego; Early Learning games; a selection of fluffy toys. Ironic, really.

'Can I help you?' She looks up and I meet her gaze. And for a moment I see something in her eyes. Some sort of instinctive recognition maybe, even though we've never met. She knows what I'm going to say before I even open my mouth.

> '*Being with you is like eating apple pie and custard*'

'I bet he told you his wife was an old bag who didn't satisfy him any more,' I say quietly. 'I bet he told you she didn't appreciate him – all the old clichés. But here I am – the same age as you, although not quite as obvious, maybe.'

She draws back – is she afraid I'm going to lean across the fluffy toys and slap her? It's tempting, but that's not why I'm here.

'I didn't...' she begins.

'What? Know he was married? Really!' It isn't a question and anyway I don't believe her. Everyone knows everyone in the table-top sale community. It's like an extended family – the stall holders look out for each other. That's how I found out about her – a quiet word from a concerned 'friend'. 'Please don't shoot the messenger, Leanne,' she had said, 'But there's something I think you should know.'

'He won't leave me,' I say to Eton Mess Woman, with a confidence I don't feel. 'And you're not the first. Don't think that for a minute.'

Her cheeks turn redder – she doesn't want this confrontation, not here amid her new contemporaries. She might have been able to handle a secret affair, but she doesn't want to be a public scarlet woman.

I have said my piece. I leave, spinning around, my pride intact, if not my heart. Mission accomplished. I am a hundred per cent sure that at next month's sale there will be an empty table.

Fifteen minutes later I pull up outside my mum's. I need to gather myself. I need to calm down, cool my flushed cheeks. I hate confrontations, too, and that was one of the hardest things I've ever had to do.

I walk up to the front door and ring the bell. I feel calmer now. Purged.

Of course, I don't know for sure whether Dad will ever stray again – I think not. You see, I lied to his Eton Mess lady in more ways than one. He never has before. He's as solid as fruit cake, my dad. Having Beth so late in life was a shock to him, it was all too much, he wanted the single life again, and he went a bit mad. He was flattered when Gina – that's Eton Mess lady – offered herself on a plate, so to speak. I know he really misses Mum, though, since he moved out, because that's what he told me when I confronted him. I know that deep down he and Mum are solid, too.

She doesn't know about Gina, though I think she has her suspicions. My mum is the kindest, most trusting, most gentle person in the world.

I want to tell her that she doesn't need to worry any more – that the way is clear for them to move on. I can't do that, of course. I suspect that what will actually happen is that I will play with my little sister, Beth, while Mum makes us a cuppa. After a bit, Mum and I will sit at the kitchen table and chat about trivia. She will get shop-bought cake from the cupboard, she hasn't time these days to make any from scratch, and then – maybe not today, but soon – my dad will phone to ask if he can come home.

THE END
© *Della Galton, 2013*

15 Monday

16 Tuesday

17 Wednesday

18 Thursday

19 Friday

20 Saturday

21 Sunday

Take a... Teacup

...and give it a whole new purpose

Floral Display

A teacup makes a delightful alternative to a vase for a little posy or a single bloom

Select pretty cups and saucers, vintage or modern, fill with flowers, and arrange them in a cluster to create a stunning centrepiece for a table. Alternatively, place them in a row along a mantelpiece or shelf – individual teacups will look lovely, too. To hold the flowers in position, cut florist's foam to fit inside each cup, soak the foam, then arrange your flowers.

● Shown above: 1990 Hartington Lane (top left); 1920 Spring Meadow (top right); 1930 Polka Rose (centre left), all by Royal Albert (01782 404045; royalalbert.co.uk). Antique teacup (upper right), stylist's own. V&A Brompton Rose (upper middle), discontinued but try China Search (01926 512402; chinasearch.co.uk). Wedgwood Cuckoo Pink (centre right), by Wedgwood (01782 282320; wedgwood.co.uk).

Make A Stand

Create a stunning cake stand from vintage crockery

Choose an assortment of dinner, cake or side plates that work well together and that vary in size. When choosing the teacups that will be turned upside down, ensure the cup handle doesn't stand above the cup rim, so it will stick to the flat surface of the plate. Make sure plates are free from grease and dust, and prepare some ceramic adhesive following the manufacturer's instructions. Hold each cup in the centre of a plate and mark its position with a chinagraph pencil. Mark the centre of the plates – so the cups are glued centrally. Apply the glue to both surfaces and hold in place until bonded. Wipe any excess glue away quickly with a damp cloth.

● *Plates and cups from a selection at Hampton Court Emporium (020 8941 9032). Evo-Stick Epoxy Rapid Syringe, Homebase (0845 640 7079; homebase.co.uk). Cakes, Delicious Moments (07985 718645; deliciousmomentscakes.co.uk).*

Making Your Garden Grow

Got a few minutes (or an hour) to spare? Choose from Adrienne Wild's straightforward summer jobs

If you only have...

10 Minutes

Spray roses with soapy water to wash off aphids.

Plant out dahlia plants. If you're growing tall varieties, support them with a stake driven into the ground.

Harden off half-hardy plants by taking them outside during the day and bringing them back under cover at night. Do this for seven to 10 days before planting out in the garden.

Propagate pinks. Take cuttings of non-flowering shoots about 4in long and push them into pots of gritty compost.

Sow seed of wallflowers in a corner of the garden to transplant in autumn, interweaving them with tulip bulbs for a beautiful display of blooms next spring.

15 Minutes

Trim lavender, cutting off the old blooms and about 15cm of the current year's growth.

Cut down early-flowering perennials, such as lupins and delphiniums, to tidy them and encourage a second flush of flowers later in the year.

40 Minutes

Clip hedges of *Lonicera nitida* and privet regularly throughout summer to maintain shape. Lay down a sheet to catch clippings. They'll rot quicker if you can shred them before you compost them.

20 Minutes

Tie in climbing and rambling roses, laying the stems horizontally to encourage more blooms.

Lift spring bulbs to make room for summer bedding plants. If the weather is dry, water the soil thoroughly before planting.

Cut the lawn twice a week to produce a thick sward. If the weather is dry, raise the height of the cut slightly and remove the cutting box.

Plant out tender bedding plants, either in pots and containers or directly in borders, watering them in with a weak solution of liquid feed.

Plant out dahlias and chrysanthemums raised from cuttings, giving each a strong stake to support the flower stems as they grow.

22 Monday

23 Tuesday

24 Wednesday

25 Thursday

26 Friday

27 Saturday

28 Sunday

JULY

29 Monday

30 Tuesday

1 Wednesday

2 Thursday

3 Friday

4 Saturday

5 Sunday

You will need

- Blue, turquoise, red, white, black, yellow and brown 5mm-wide quilling papers
- Grey 3mm-wide quilling paper
- Quilling tool
- Cocktail stick
- PVA glue
- Tracing paper and sharp HB pencil
- 9.5 x 13cm rectangle of light-blue card
- Masking tape
- Paper scissors
- Ruler
- Tweezers
- A5 piece of light-blue checked card

Pack of 100 x 5mm quilling papers in assorted colours; set of three quilling tools, both from a selection at Fred Aldous (0161 236 4224; fredaldous.co.uk).

Have A Go At...
Quilling

The papercraft that's fun, easy and looks impressive

Quilling is simply rolling up strips of coloured paper to create 3D designs. You can use different widths of paper and shape the rolls into squares, triangles, ovals or even teardrop and heart shapes.

Quilling paper strips are available in 3mm, 5mm and 1cm widths, or you can cut your own from a sheet of paper using a craft knife against a metal ruler on a cutting mat. The best weight paper to use is 100gsm.

Quilling tools have a protruding dowel with a slot into which you slip your paper strip to start coiling. The tools are available with slots of different depths to match the width of paper, but it is possible to use any width paper in any depth of slot. The protruding dowels also differ in width, so you can vary the size of the hole at the centre of the coil. If you don't have a quilling tool, improvise by wrapping the strip around a cocktail stick.

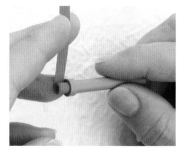

1 Practise rolling the quilling paper into coils using a quilling tool. Insert one end of the paper into the slot, then twirl the tool with one hand to wind the paper into a tight coil. Slip the coil off the tool. To secure a tight coil, use a cocktail stick to apply a dab of glue to the open end. To make a relaxed coil, leave it to loosen, then glue the end in place. Experiment with relaxed coils to form different shapes: pinch one side to make a teardrop, or pinch at opposite sides to make an oval shape or all four sides to make a square.

block and one 20cm length of red quilling paper for the bottom block. Make a relaxed coil for each, gluing the ends in place. To make the blocks into squares, pinch the coils at opposite sides, release, then pinch at opposite sides halfway between the first folds. Shape them into squares. Arrange the blocks within the casing, then glue them in place.

2 Trace the lighthouse template *(below right)* onto tracing paper with a sharp pencil. Use masking tape to stick the tracing face down 4.5cm above the centre of the lower straight edge of the light-blue card. Redraw the lighthouse to transfer the design, then remove the tracing. Make four blue and three turquoise relaxed coils from 10cm lengths of quilling paper; don't glue the ends. To turn them into waves, wrap the ends around a cocktail stick a couple of times in the opposite direction. Lay a ruler across the card 2cm above the lower straight edge. Arrange the blue waves in a row across the centre of the card with the lower edges butted against the ruler. Glue the waves in place. Next, place the ruler across the card 3cm above the lower edge. Glue one turquoise wave at the centre, with the upper edge butted against the ruler and the remaining two either side.

4 Cut two 10cm lengths of black quilling paper and make relaxed coils. Pinch one coil at opposite sides to make a leaf shape. Squeeze the leaf flat and glue to the top of the lighthouse as a balcony. To make the lamp, make a square from a 15cm length of yellow quilling paper as described in step 3. Glue the lamp above the balcony. Pinch the other black coil at three places to make a triangle, glue above the lamp as the roof. Make a tight coil from a 5cm length of black quilling paper and glue to the top of the roof.

5 Make relaxed coils from three 15cm lengths of brown quilling paper. Gently squeeze the coils to make ovals for the rocks. Glue the rocks between the waves and lighthouse. Fold two 3.5cm lengths of grey quilling paper in half for the

gulls. Pull the ends of the paper between a thumb and finger to curl them. Cut off 5mm at one end of one gull wing. Arrange the gulls on the card, then glue in place.

6 Fold the A5 piece of card in half to form a greetings card. Open out and lay flat on a surface with right side facing upwards. Glue quilling design centrally to the right-hand side. Allow to dry, then refold into a card.

Actual-sized template for lighthouse

3 Cut a 7cm length of red quilling paper for the lighthouse casing. Fold the paper 3cm from both ends. Run a line of glue along the outline of the lighthouse on the card using a cocktail stick. Stick the casing along the glued line, matching the folds to the corners. Cut one 15cm length of red quilling paper for the top block, one 18cm length of white quilling paper for the middle

Would you like to do more quilling?
Then check out womansweekly. co.uk for step-by-step instructions on how to make this fantastic ice-cream card.

POST – CARD

Reader Samantha Priestley, from Sothall, South Yorkshire, nominates the Tinside Lido in Plymouth, Devon

'This beautiful salt-water swimming pool was built in 1935 and restored to its original art-deco design in 2003. Stretching out into the sea, this amazing lido is fun for all the family and sits in the Plymouth Hoe, near where Sir Francis Drake is supposed to have played bowls before the arrival of the Spanish Armada.'

6 Monday

7 Tuesday

8 Wednesday

9 Thursday

10 Friday

11 Saturday

12 Sunday

Gala Slice

Serves 6-8
Calories: 440
Fat: 31g
Saturated fat: 12g
Suitable for freezing: ✗

1 Remove the skin from all the sausages, put the meat in a bowl and mix in the chopped spring onions and plenty of salt and freshly ground black pepper.

2 Cut the pastry block in half. Roll out one piece to a rectangle 38 x 13cm (15 x 5in) or as long as will fit on your baking sheet. Put the pastry on the lined baking sheet. Spread the mustard over to within 2cm (¾in) of the edges.

3 Spread a third of the meat mixture down the middle, on the mustard. Place the boiled eggs on top, butting them together. Mould the rest of the meat mixture around the eggs. It's easier if your hands are wet. Brush the pastry edges with beaten egg.

4 Roll out the leftover pastry to a rectangle 43 x 18cm (17 x 7in) and lay it carefully over the top of the meat and egg filling. Ease it over and seal around it well, then trim the edges and decorate them.

5 Chill the slice while the oven heats up to 200°C or Gas Mark 6. Brush the pastry with beaten egg. Score the top, then bake it for 45 minutes. Leave for 10 minutes before slicing. Serve sliced, warm or cold, with salad.

* 600g (1¼lb) of your favourite pork sausages (9 sausages)
* 6 spring onions, trimmed and chopped
* 375g pack Jus-Rol All-Butter Puff Pastry
* 1 tablespoon ready-made English mustard
* 6 medium eggs, hard-boiled (boil for 6-8 minutes)
* 1 medium egg, beaten

* *Large baking tray, lined with baking parchment*

Tip from our kitchen

Use sausage meat if you prefer, but we find it tends to be fattier than good-quality sausages. Add fresh or dried herbs or spices to the mixture if you want to give it extra flavour.

Your Good Health

Ask Dr Mel

Q I keep getting attacks of hives and have to take antihistamines most of the time; it's turning into a real irritation. What causes this?

A Hives, or urticaria, is very common, but fewer than one in 200 people get it regularly.

The itchy red rash and raised white blotches look like nettlerash and develop when histamine and other chemicals are released in the skin. This can be triggered by allergies to foods such as shellfish, nuts or strawberries, insect stings, infections, medication such as penicillin, aspirin, morphine-related drugs or ACE-inhibitors (for hypertension), or even cold, heat or pressure.

But in chronic urticaria, it's often hard to identify the cause (although it may be an attack by the body's own immune system). It sometimes leads to angioedema (fluid and swelling in the skin tissues), and occasionally to potentially fatal swelling of the eyes, lips, tongue and throat (if so, call 999 immediately).

Antihistamines tend to be effective for minor or infrequent reactions, but you may need to see an immunologist to see if the cause can be identified and removed. 'Stronger' treatments include steroids, antileukotrienes, type 2 antihistamines, such as ranitidine, and the newer, immunosuppressant drug, omalizumab.

TAKE 5...
Tips For A Good Night's Sleep

1 MAKE SURE your bedroom is comfortable, quiet and dark.

2 AVOID daytime catch-up' naps if you suffer from insomnia.

3 WIND YOUR BRAIN down – avoid late-night computers, e-mails, texting, and stimulating TV.

4 IF YOU'RE NOT ASLEEP within 20 minutes of going to bed, get up and try again later.

5 KEEP REGULAR habits – always get up and go to bed around the same time each night.

A Great Exercise To...
Work all the major muscle groups
– core, legs, hips, chest, arms, back and shoulders

Jumping Jacks

Stand with feet together, arms by your sides. Bend the knees slightly and jump just a few inches into the air. As you do so bring your legs out and raise your arms over your head. Land with your feet shoulder-width apart, hands meeting above your head. Immediately jump your feet back to the start position, with arms down.

Start with five, then progress to 10 and more. *Well done!*

TIP Doing a few loosening-up stretches before you start will improve flexibility and reduce any risk of injury. Simply stand straight and shake arms and legs for about a minute.

HOW THE EXPERTS STAY HEALTHY
Jayne Morris, life coach

What's in your medicine cabinet?
I take an immune-system booster supplement daily, to prevent coughs and colds.

What's good in your fridge?
Japanese miso paste. I mix it with water to make a light soup, or I spread it on toast or add it to eggs, fish, mushrooms or tofu. Yum!

What's your favourite exercise?
Martial arts, but with a baby it's tricky to get to evening classes, so I use a Tae-bo DVD.

What's a real foodie treat?
Home-made banana bread with ice cream.

What makes you happy?
Being with people who love what they do and do what they love.

What's the secret of a good night's sleep?
Disconnecting from e-mails and text messages at least an hour before bed.

What stresses you out and how do you cope?
Too much to do in too little time. I focus on the most important thing and forget the rest.

Are there any remedies from your childhood that you still use?
A hot-water bottle and cucumber sandwiches always make me feel better.
● Visit jaynemorris.com

13 Monday

14 Tuesday

15 Wednesday

16 Thursday

17 Friday

18 Saturday

19 Sunday

Added Interest

Cable edging and toggle fasteners lift this adorable jacket out of the ordinary

- Easy-peasy
- A Bit More Tricky
- **Hard-ish**
- Quite A Challenge

MEASUREMENTS

To fit ages 1 (1½) (2) (3) (4) years.
Actual chest measurements
66 (70) (73) (76) (79.5) cm/
26 (27½) (28¾) (30) (31¼) in.
Side seam 17 (18.5) (20) (21.5) (23) cm/6¾ (7¼) (7¾) (8½) (9) in.
Length to shoulder 27.5 (30) (32.5) (35) (37.5) cm/10¾ (11¾) (12¾) (13¾) (14¾) in.
Sleeve seam 17 (19) (20.5) (21.5) (25.5) cm/6¾ (7½) (8) (8½) (10) in.

MATERIALS

4 (5) (6) (6) (7) 50g balls of Sublime Extra Fine Merino Wool DK (100% wool) in Holiday (350). Pair of 4mm (No. 8) knitting needles; cable needle; 4 toggles.
You can buy the yarn online at womansweeklyshop.com/yarn or call 0800 024 1212.

TENSION

22 stitches and 28 rows, to 10 x 10cm, over stocking stitch, using 4mm needles.

ABBREVIATIONS

K, knit; **p**, purl; **st**, stitch; **tog**, together; **inc**, increase (by working twice into same st); **dec**, decrease (by taking 2 sts tog); **rss**, reverse stocking st (k on right side and p on wrong side); **sl**, slip; **c4**, cable 4 (sl next 2 sts on to cable needle and leave at back, k2, then k2 from cable needle); **ytf**, yarn to front; **ytb**, yarn to back; **nil**, meaning nothing is worked here for this size.

NOTE

Yarn amounts are based on average requirements and are therefore approximate. Instructions are given for small size. Where they vary, work figures in round brackets for larger sizes. Instructions in square brackets are worked as stated after 2nd bracket.

CABLE PANEL

Worked over 23 sts.
1st row: K4, [p2, k4] 3 times, p1.
2nd row: K1, [p4, k2] 3 times, p4.
3rd row: K4, [p2, k4] 3 times, p1.
4th row: K1, [p4, k2] 3 times, p4.
5th row: C4, [p2, c4] 3 times, p1.
6th row: K1, [p4, k2] 3 times, p4.

BACK AND FRONTS

Knitted sideways in one piece.
Right front: With 4mm needles,
cast on 64 (67) (72) (75) (81) sts for
front edge.
1st row: P to last 23 sts, work 5th
(3rd) (5th) (1st) (5th) row of panel.
2nd row: Work 6th (4th) (6th) (2nd)
(6th) row of panel, k to end.
These 2 rows set position of panel.
Working the panel pattern over
23 sts at lower edge as set and
remainder in rss, continue thus:
Pattern 4 (2) (3) (2) (2) rows.
Shape neck: Inc and work into rss,
1 st at beginning (beginning) (end)
(beginning) (beginning) of next row
and at same edge on following 5 (7)
(7) (9) (9) rows – 70 (75) (80) (85) (91)
sts. Work 1 row.
** Place marker at top edge of last
row.
Shape raglan armhole: Dec 1 st at
end (end) (beginning) (end) (end) of
next row and at same (armhole)
edge on following 2 rows, then work
1 row straight.
Repeat last 4 rows, 6 (6) (5) (4) (4)
times more – 49 (54) (62) (70) (76) sts.
Dec 1 st at armhole edge on next 3
(5) (10) (15) (17) rows – 46 (49) (52)
(55) (59) sts.
Pattern another 3 rows.
Back: Pattern 2 rows.
Shape raglan armhole: Inc 1 st at
armhole edge on next 3 (5) (10) (15)
(17) rows – 49 (54) (62) (70) (76) sts.
Pattern 1 row straight. Inc 1 st at
armhole edge on next 3 rows.
Repeat last 4 rows, 6 (6) (5) (4)
(4) times more – 70 (75) (80) (85)
(91) sts.
Place marker at top edge of last row.
**
Back neck: Pattern another 27 (29)
(31) (33) (35) rows.
Work from ** to **, reading left front
instead of back. Pattern 1 row.
Shape neck: Dec 1 st at neck edge on
next 6 (8) (8) (10) (10) rows – 64 (67)
(72) (75) (81) sts.

Pattern another 6 (4) (5) (4) (4) rows.
Cast off.

SLEEVES (both alike)

With 4mm needles, cast on 5 (9) (7)
(5) (13) sts. K 1 row and p 1 row.
**Shape seam and raglan top: Next
row:** Cast on 5 sts, k to last st, inc in
last st.
Next row: Inc in first st, p to end.
Repeat last 2 rows, 3 (3) (4) (5) (5)
times more. **Next row:** Cast on 23 sts,
work 2nd (6th) (2nd) (6th) (2nd) row
of panel, k to last st, inc in last st – 57
(61) (66) (71) (79) sts.
Working panel pattern over the 23
sts at lower edge as set and
remainder in rss, continue thus: Inc 1
st at raglan edge on next 15 (17) (14)
(8) (13) rows – 72 (78) (80) (79) (92) sts.
3rd, 4th and 5th sizes only: Work 1
row. Inc 1 st at raglan edge on next
3 rows. Repeat last 4 rows, nil (2) (1)
time(s) more – 83 (88) (98) sts.
All sizes: Mark raglan edge of last
row. Pattern 11 rows. Mark raglan
edge of last row.
3rd, 4th and 5th sizes only: Dec 1 st
at raglan edge on next 3 rows, then
work 1 row straight.
Repeat last 4 rows, nil (2) (1) time(s)
more – 80 (79) (92) sts.
All sizes: Dec 1 st at raglan edge on
next 15 (17) (14) (8) (13) rows – 57
(61) (66) (71) (79) sts.
Next row: Cast off 23 sts, k to last 2
sts, k2tog. **Next row:** P2tog, p to end.
Next row: Cast off 5 sts, k to last 2 sts,
k2tog. Repeat last 2 rows, 3 (3) (4) (5)
(5) times more – 5 (9) (7) (5) (13) sts.
Rss 2 rows. Cast off.

HOOD

With 4mm needles, cast on 23 sts.
Work 1st and 2nd rows of panel.
Next row: Cast on 4 (4) (5) (5) (5) sts,
p4 (4) (5) (5) (5), work 3rd row of
panel. **Next row:** Work 4th row of
panel, k to end.
Working panel pattern over the 23
sts at face edge as set and remainder
in rss, continue thus: Cast on 4 (4) (5)
(5) (5) sts at beginning of next row
and following alternate row.
Pattern 1 row. Cast on 8 (10) (9) (10)
(12) sts at beginning of next row –
43 (45) (47) (48) (50) sts.
Pattern 1 row. Mark end of last row.
Inc 1 st at beginning of next row and
3 (3) (3) (4) (4) following alternate

rows, then on 2 following 4th rows
– 49 (51) (53) (55) (57) sts.
Pattern another 33 (39) (45) (49) (55)
rows.
Dec 1 st at beginning of next row
and 3 following alternate rows, then
at same edge on next 2 rows – 43
(45) (47) (49) (51) sts.
Shape top: Next 2 rows: Pattern 23,
ytb, sl1, ytf, turn, sl1, pattern to end.
Next 2 rows: Pattern 29 (30) (31) (31)
(32), ytf, sl1, ytb, turn, sl1, pattern to
end. **Next 2 rows:** Pattern 35 (37) (39)
(39) (41), ytf, sl1, ytb, turn, sl1, pattern
to end.
Pattern 2 rows across all sts.
Next 2 rows: Pattern 35 (37) (39) (39)
(41), ytf, sl1, ytb, turn, sl1, pattern to
end. **Next 2 rows:** Pattern 29 (30) (31)
(31) (32), ytf, sl1, ytb, turn, sl1, pattern
to end. **Next 2 rows:** Pattern 23, ytb,
sl1, ytf, turn, sl1, pattern to end.
Next row: Pattern to last st, inc in
last st.
Inc 1 st at beginning of next row and
at same edge on following row, then
on 3 following alternate rows – 49
(51) (53) (55) (57) sts.
Pattern another 33 (39) (45) (49) (55)
rows.
Dec 1 st at end of next row and 2
following 4th rows, then on 3 (3) (3)
(4) (4) following alternate rows – 43
(45) (47) (48) (50) sts.
Mark end of last row.
Cast off 8 (10) (9) (10) (12) sts at
beginning of next row and 4 (4) (5)
(5) (5) sts at beginning of 3 following
alternate rows – 23 sts. Pattern 2
rows. Cast off.

FRONT EDGING (both alike)

With right side facing and using
4mm needles, pick up and k42 (46)
(52) (54) (57) sts along front edge.
K 2 rows. Cast off kwise.

TO MAKE UP

Join sleeve seams. Matching markers
on top edges, sew in sleeves. Fold
hood in half lengthways and join
back seam from folded edge to
markers. Sew hood in position. Using
4 strands of yarn together, make 2
twisted cords, each 20cm long. Tie
ends together on each cord to form
toggle loop. Twist loops into figure
8 and secure at centre. Position and
sew centre of loops to left front. Sew
on toggles.

Woman Overboard!

This holiday had become a habit. Was their marriage just a habit, too?

Evelyn tutted. Then tutted again, louder this time. At the third tut the woman in the floaty dress and pashmina turned round. Evelyn looked down to her lap, as though she hadn't tutted at all.

Roger sighed. Why did she always do that? Either she wanted people to know they were annoying her or she didn't.

'She's not the only one,' Evelyn said.

'Not the only one what?' asked Roger.

'Who wants to see the view. Why doesn't she sit down, instead of standing at the rail and getting in everyone's way? We've all come on this boat trip for the same reason, haven't we? To enjoy the view and – A BIT OF PEACE AND QUIET.'

The increased volume of the final phrase caused Roger to follow the direction of her stare to a young man with an iPod.

'What is the point of earphones if we can all hear the racket?' Evelyn asked.

'He's young,' said Roger.

'He's old enough to have learned some respect,' said Evelyn. 'It's a gaudy frock, don't you think, for someone of that age?'

After a moment, Roger realised they were back on the floaty-dress woman and the mental image he had formed of the young man in a frock faded.

'I expect it's cool in this heat,' Roger said.

A sudden guffaw of laughter from a large gentleman with a mobile phone against his ear started another round of tutting from Evelyn.

'You can hear every word,' she said.

'But you can't understand it,' said Roger. 'He's German, I think, from the accent.'

'That's not the point,' Evelyn said.

So little of what he said was these days, Roger thought.

'Shall I get us some drinks?' he asked, not wishing to follow the path where his thoughts were taking him. A beer would go down nicely. 'There's a bar inside.'

'Water,' Evelyn said. 'You don't want to be drinking beer in this heat.'

Oh, well.

They'd been here on holiday many times. In the early years they had travelled all over, then gradually they had come here every third year, then every second and now they never went anywhere else.

It had become a habit, like so many things. Was their marriage just a habit, too?

Roger returned with the water and handed a bottle to Evelyn.

She took it from him and unscrewed the top without comment.

'It's still beautiful, isn't it?' he said softly.

'Yes,' Evelyn said.

'Shall I take a photo? You and the view?'

'We've got lots like that already.'

'Not from this year, not of you today.'

'I haven't changed,' said Evelyn.

Oh, but she had.

When they had both been working they had savoured every minute of their trips. He'd retired three years before and had slipped easily into a life of reading and

'He's German, I think, from the accent'

gardening. Evelyn had retired earlier in the year and hadn't been the same since.

Roger had hoped that this trip back to their favourite place would bring back the old Evelyn, but if anything she was worse.

The woman in the floaty dress was at it again, leaning over the rail, laughing as the probably-German man took her photo.

Evelyn leaned to one side then the other, trying to see the view, then stood up sharply.

'I will have my photo taken,' she said to Roger. 'Over there, by the rail.'

'But...'

'It's not her boat. I've as much right.' She stormed over to where the other woman stood and glared at her until she moved.

Roger reached down into the bag for the camera as Evelyn leaned back against the rail posing for the shot. He looked up just in time to see her feet slip from under her as she went backwards into the water.

There was a loud splash.

Roger froze. 'Oh!' he said. 'My wife!'

The rest seemed to happen all at once.

A blur of denim passed before his eyes and there was another splash.

He saw floaty-dress woman rushing to the front of the boat.

He could hear a loud voice shouting into a phone: 'Ja. Schnell. Ambulance.'

The boat turned round and he saw Evelyn on her back in the water, safe in the arms of iPod boy.

They were hauled aboard by strong probably-German arms. Evelyn was shivering despite the heat and a pashmina appeared around her shoulders.

Her denim-clad saviour was shaking the water out of his iPod.

Then Evelyn started crying. 'I'm sorry,' she said. 'I'm sorry.'

* * *

Back at the hotel, Roger and Evelyn sat on their balcony. Paramedics waiting at the quayside had declared Evelyn to be fine, despite her ordeal. There had, however, been many more tears.

'What is the point of me now?' Evelyn had asked. 'I used to be someone. People looked up to me. Now, I'm just...'

And Roger had finally understood. 'You're you,' he said. 'You're my Evelyn.'

And they had talked, at last, about how their life together had changed and how it could be an even better life than before.

'Maybe we should go somewhere else next year,' Evelyn said now.

'Maybe,' Roger said. 'But it is lovely here. We could possibly stretch to both.'

'Keep some old things, add some new?'

'Sounds good to me,' Roger said, and he smiled as he sipped the beer he had finally been allowed.

'I was horrible about those people,' Evelyn said, 'and they helped me. I've learned a lesson there.'

Roger said nothing. Although some things had changed, it was still as well for a husband to know when to bite his tongue.

THE END

© Bernadette James, 2013

20 Monday

21 Tuesday

22 Wednesday

23 Thursday

24 Friday

25 Saturday

26 Sunday

All Lit Up

Fill small tins with wax to create a row of unusual, colourful candles

Eat the contents, then turn pretty sweet tins into candles – it's very simple, though do be careful with hot wax. Carefully melt your wax following the manufacturer's instructions, either in the microwave, or in a bowl suspended over a saucepan of boiling water. Position a wick in the base of each tin, then – using a jug – pour in the hot liquid wax. Fill to the brim, then secure the wick in the centre by tying a skewer on either side of it, resting on top of the tin. Before the wax sets completely, pierce any bubbles that appear and top up with more wax.

● *We used: Leone sugared sweets collection (pack of 6), from a selection at The Conran Shop (0844 848 4000; conranshop.co.uk). Yaley pre-waxed wire wick and clip (pack of 12); premium wax pellets 454g, both from a selection at Hobbycraft (01202 596100; hobbycraft.co.uk).*

*Never leave a burning candle unattended

27 Monday

28 Tuesday

29 Wednesday

30 Thursday

31 Friday

1 Saturday

2 Sunday

Quick Crossword

Simply fill in the crossword and unscramble the letters in the shaded squares to reveal the name of a flowering shrub (8).

ACROSS

1 Hanging embroidery such as that at Bayeux (8)
5 Apple seeds (4)
9 Spacious (5)
10 Admire to an extreme degree (7)
11 Healing ointment (4)
12 Bible stands (8)
14 Yapped like a dog (6)
15 Make unhappy (6)
18 Sofa which converts to a bed (3-3-2)
20 Deliberately disobey (4)
23 Unauthorised by law (7)
24 Sarcastic, nasty (remark) (5)
25 Active volcano in eastern Sicily (4)
26 Made bigger (8)

DOWN

1 Beat violently (of the heart) (5)
2 Person lurking suspiciously (7)
3 Eyelid infection (4)
4 Drizzled or teemed (6)
6 Chillier (5)
7 Wide-brimmed cowboy-style hat (7)
8 Mail deliverer (7)
13 Feel delight, make merry (7)
14 Christen (7)
16 Controlling calories (7)
17 Flesh of sheep as food (6)
19 Bird of prey's sharp claw (5)
21 Give way or surrender (5)
22 Continent (4)

You can work it out...

Solutions to this month's puzzle on September puzzles

SOLUTIONS FOR JUNE 2015

Answer: YORKSHIRE

AUGUST

Go Potty
For Flowers

A simple-knit pot of blooms that will always look bright and beautiful

Easy-peasy

A Bit More
Tricky

Hard-ish

Quite A
Challenge

MEASUREMENTS
19cm/7½in high.

MATERIALS
1 x 50g ball of Rico Design Creative Cotton Aran (100% cotton) in each of Nougat (56), Pistachio (41), Red (05), Orange (74), Light Yellow (63), and Fuchsia (13). Pair of 4mm (No. 8) knitting needles. Washable toy stuffing.
You can buy the yarn online at womansweeklyshop.com/yarn or call 0800 024 1212.

TENSION
20 stitches and 28 rows, to 10 x 10cm, over stocking stitch using 4mm needles.

ABBREVIATIONS
K, knit; **p**, purl; **st**, stitch; **sl**, slip; **tog**, together; **dec**, decrease (by taking 2 sts tog); **inc**, increase (by working twice into same st); **ss**, stocking st (k on right side and p on wrong side); **rss**, reverse stocking st (p on right side and k on wrong side).

NOTE
Instructions in square brackets are worked as stated after 2nd bracket.

FLOWERPOT
With 4mm needles and Nougat, cast on 12 sts. P 1 row.
1st inc row: Inc kwise in each st – 24 sts. P 1 row. **2nd inc row:** [Inc in next st, k1] to end – 36 sts. P 1 row. **3rd inc row:** [Inc in next st, k2] to end – 48 sts. P 1 row. **4th inc row:** [Inc in next st, k3] to end – 60 sts. P 1 row. P 1 row for base edge.
Beginning with a p row, ss 5 rows.
5th inc row: [Inc in next st, k9] to end – 66 sts. Ss 11 rows.
6th inc row: [Inc in next st, k10] to end – 72 sts. Ss 5 rows.
Beginning with a p row, rss 8 rows.
Change to Pistachio and k 2 rows.
1st dec row: [K10, k2tog] to end –

66 sts. K 3 rows. **2nd dec row:** [K9, k2tog] to end – 60 sts. K 3 rows.
3rd dec row: [K8, k2tog] to end – 54 sts. K 1 row. **4th dec row:** [K7, k2tog] to end – 48 sts. K 1 row.
5th dec row: [K6, k2tog] to end – 42 sts. K 1 row. **6th dec row:** [K5, k2tog] to end – 36 sts. K 1 row.
7th dec row: [K2, k2tog] to end – 27 sts. K 1 row. **8th dec row:** [K1, k2tog] to end – 18 sts. K 1 row.
9th dec row: [K2tog] to end – 9 sts.
Break off yarn, thread end through remaining sts, pull up tightly and secure.Gather cast-on edge, pull up tightly and secure. Join row-ends together leaving an opening. Stuff firmly and close opening.

DAISY
Petals (make 2): With 4mm needles and Light Yellow, cast on 4 sts.
1st row: Inc kwise in first st, k2, turn. **2nd row:** Sl1, p3.
3rd row: K2, turn. **4th row:** Sl1, p1.
5th row: Cast off 4 sts, sl st used in casting-off back onto left-hand needle, cast on 3 sts.
Repeat 1st to 5th rows, 3 times more, then work 1st to 4th rows again.
Cast off.
Gather straight edge of each piece, pull up tightly and secure. Place pieces of petals together, making sure that petals of top layer are between petals of lower layer and secure in position. With

Pistachio, work French knot at centre of each daisy.
Make another daisy in Light Yellow and 2 in each of Red, Orange and Fuchsia.

LARGE ROSE
With 4mm needles and Light Yellow, cast on 7 sts.
1st row: Inc kwise in first st, k5, turn.
2nd row: P7.
3rd row: K6, turn. **4th row:** Sl1, p5.
5th row: K. **6th row:** P. **7th row:** K4, turn. **8th row:** Sl1, p3.
Repeat 3rd to 8th rows, 4 times more, then work 3rd to 5th rows again. Cast off.
With purl side on the outside, begin at cast-on edge and roll piece into rose shape. Catch down cast-off edge.
Make another large rose in Light Yellow and 2 in each of Red, Orange and Fuchsia.

SMALL ROSE
With 4mm needles and Light Yellow, cast on 4 sts.
1st row: Inc kwise in first st, k2, turn.
2nd row: P4. **3rd row:** K3, turn. **4th row:** Sl1, p2. **5th row:** K. **6th row:** P.
7th row: K4, turn. **8th row:** Sl1, p3.
Repeat 3rd to 8th rows, twice more, then work 3rd to 5th rows again.
Cast off.
With purl side on the outside, begin at cast-on edge and roll piece into rose shape. Catch down cast-off edge.
Make 2 more small roses in each of Red, Orange and Fuchsia.

TO COMPLETE
Arrange flowers on top of pot and sew them in place.

Let's Go Down To The Lido

A better diet and more opportunities to exercise plus advances in drugs made a huge and positive impact on the health of the nation

OH, life is so full of
Sad troubles and snares!
I smelt hot, new buns, and
I fell down the stairs!

Chew on this…

Two mothers' concerns, swiftly dealt with by Matron, in 1931

For a choking child: 'Try smacking the child between the shoulders. If that does not succeed, hook out the piece of food with your finger from the back of the throat. In obstinate cases…hold him upside down by the feet and slap his back.'

Baby's vaccination: 'It does not give any pain at the time, no more than a tiny scratch from a pin. Sometimes, babies become a little fretful on the fourth day. Sips of cooled boiled water and attention to proper evacuation of the bowels gets them through this temporary discomfort.'

A tot who spoke for all children Little Bill was our toddler poet – voiced by the accomplished children's author, Irene Heath – who expressed the joy, confusion and frustration of finding his way in the world

The great outdoors The value of open-air exercise as an all-round cure was recognised and promoted for everyone – it was a craze we happily took to

3 Monday

4 Tuesday

5 Wednesday

6 Thursday

7 Friday

8 Saturday

9 Sunday

Coming Up Roses

Fabulously floral things for the bedroom – and great gifts, if you can bear to part with them!

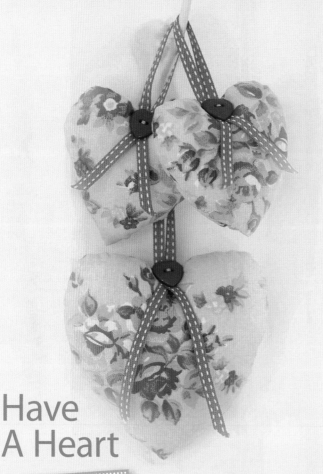

Have A Heart

- Rico Flowers Red Rose fabric
- Soft polyester toy filling
- Heart-shaped buttons
- 6mm-wide ribbon
- Matching sewing thread and needle

1 Enlarge the image of the larger heart (left) by 170% for a large heart (120% for a small heart). Cut two 20cm-square pieces of fabric and place them right sides together. Trace on the heart shape; cut out.

2 Taking a 5mm seam allowance, machine-stitch all around the heart, leaving a 3cm opening for turning through. Turn right side out and press.

3 Stuff the heart evenly with the toy filling, then hand-stitch the opening closed.

4 Loop a 30cm piece of ribbon and stitch to the top centre of the heart, trimming the ends diagonally. Then stitch a heart-shaped button to the centre of the loop.

Safe Keeping

- Two 50 x 26cm pieces of Rico Flowers Red Rose fabric
- 49 x 26cm piece wadding
- 6mm-wide and 15mm-wide ribbon
- 15mm clear snap fastener
- Matching sewing thread and needle

1 Stitch the 15mm ribbon across the width of one piece of fabric, 10.5cm down from the top edge. Press a 1cm seam along the bottom edge of both pieces of fabric.

2 Place the wadding on a flat surface, followed by the piece of fabric with the ribbon trim, right side up, then the other piece of fabric, right side down, and pin all three layers together.

3 Measure 8cm in from both top corners and then 8cm down

All Hung Up

Display your favourite nightie on a pretty hanger

from both top corners, and mark. Then cut diagonally through fabric and wadding, from one point to the other on both sides.

4 Machine-stitch a 1cm seam along the two long edges and along the top, leaving the lower end open.

5 Trim the wadding close to the seam, and trim the corners at the top. Turn to the right side. Turn in the lower hem and machine-stitch.

6 With the ribbon side down, turn lower end of bag up 15cm and machine-stitch along both sides. Stitch one part of the snap fastener under the top flap, then fold flap down to find the position of the other bit of the fastener. Stitch in place.

7 Tie a length of 6mm ribbon into a bow and stitch to the middle of the wider ribbon.

You will need

- ✿ **20 x 55cm Rico Flowers Red Rose fabric per hanger**
- ✿ **Abbey Easy Quilt Precut Polyester Wadding**
- ✿ **6mm-wide ribbon**
- ✿ **Satin bias binding in Rose Pink**
- ✿ **Wooden clothes hanger**
- ✿ **Matching sewing threads and needle**

1 Wrap a piece of wadding around the hanger and stitch in place to secure.

2 Cut a length of bias binding 2cm longer than the hook. Fold over a 5mm turning at one end, then fold in half lengthways. Stitch along long edge and folded end to form a tube. Slide over the hook and stitch to wadding.

3 Press a 1cm turning at both short edges of the fabric and a 2cm turning along the long edges. Mark centre points on both long edges with a pin.

4 With wrong sides facing, stitch along both short edges. Then, starting from one side of the long edge, work a running stitch 5mm down from the top edge to the centre point.

5 Slide the fabric on to the hanger, then pull the thread to gather evenly over the wadding. Stitch the other side in the same way and fasten off the thread.

6 To neaten, turn back the top outer corners diagonally and stitch to the back.

7 Tie a length of ribbon into a bow and stitch to base of hook.

● *Rico Flowers Red Rose fabric, and all other materials, from a selection at Hobbycraft (0330 026 1400; hobbycraft.co.uk).*

POST – CARD

Reader Helen Cooper, from Tenbury Wells, Worcestershire, nominates Canal D'Amour in Corfu

'Listening to waves crashing against the rocks, while watching the little lizards that scoot about, keeps me entertained for hours at Canal D'Amour. The stunning scenery takes your breath away and as well as a couple of gift shops, there's also a café-bar overlooking the sea – providing the perfect location for an enchanting, romantic evening. So it's definitely my favourite place to be!'

10 Monday

11 Tuesday

12 Wednesday

13 Thursday

14 Friday

15 Saturday

16 Sunday

Strawberry & Clotted Cream Ice Cream

Serves 6-8	
Calories: 372	
Fat: 28g	
Saturated fat: 17g	
Suitable for freezing: ✔	

* 500g (1lb) strawberries
* 200g (7oz) icing sugar
* 350g carton clotted cream
* Juice of ½ lemon

TO SERVE:
* Halved strawberries and extra clotted cream

1 Put the strawberries and icing sugar in the bowl of a food processor and whizz until smooth. Add the cream and lemon juice and whizz again until well mixed.

2 Churn the mixture in an ice-cream machine until it's frozen, or pour it into a suitable container and put it in the freezer, beating it several times while it freezes to give a smooth texture.

3 Remove the ice cream from the freezer about 15 minutes before serving, to allow it to soften for easier scooping. Serve with extra clotted cream and some halved strawberries.

✳ **The ice cream will keep in the freezer for up to 1 month.**

Tip from our kitchen

For an extra-smooth ice cream, strain the strawberry purée through a fine sieve to remove all the small pips.

Knickers

She yaps on at me in a voice that sounds just like my mother's, and she's there at every opportunity, striking fear into my heart. I try to ignore her

Knickers...

There's me.

And there's this little old lady.

She drives me mad, but I can't get away from her.

I call her Lol. Definitely not for 'laugh out loud' – she never does that. Little old lady.

She's there at every opportunity, striking fear into my heart.

'You can't do that!' she rasps, listing all the reasons that I can't – whatever that is.

It's all random. She yaps and yaps on at me in a voice that sounds just like my mother's used to.

I try to ignore her.

* * *

My brilliant idea was to jet off on an exciting holiday. Nothing to stop me, really, other than Lol. I had an urgent longing to get away from her for a bit.

I tried to keep it to myself so that she couldn't pour cold water before I'd even fixed it, but that was impossible.

'You can't go on your own!' she proclaimed.

But I couldn't see why not. All I needed to do was a bit of research, get around the travel agent's and see what was out there in that great big holiday paradise I knew nothing about.

Lol, of course, insisted on dragging herself along.

Luckily, the girl in the very first place we tried was so lovely I knew we wouldn't need to go anywhere else. Just a little slip of a thing, she was. All bright-eyed and cheerful and bubbly. I fancied a bit of cheerful and bubbly for myself. I fancied the way she had her hair streaked different shades of blonde and tied up in a cheeky little bunch.

I also fancied a bit of a trip to Europe. Somewhere sunny. Somewhere friendly. Somewhere I could just enjoy myself without having to worry about a thing.

I tried to tell Miss Bright-eyed Cheerful & Bubbly exactly what I had in mind without Lol interfering but, of course: 'Not on a coach,' she muttered at the first option. 'Sitting all that way? You won't like that!'

And: 'Then there's the ferry. What if the water's choppy? And there's hundreds of people?'

'Eurostar's comfortable,' Bright-eyes said, smiling, not perturbed in the slightest. 'And what about flying? If you go on a package you won't have a problem at all, I can find you something with a concierge...'

'That'll cost a fortune,' said Lol. 'How will you pay for it?'

'I'll manage somehow,' I said.

Bright-eyes just took no notice, showing me all the fabulous places that

'The Algarve looks just my cup of tea'

she thought were in my range.

'The Algarve looks just my cup of tea,' I mumbled.

Lol pitched in again. 'What about the heat? And the mosquitoes?'

I could feel my jaw muscles tighten every time she interrupted.

What she really made me want to do was cry uncontrollably. It felt as if my smile was crooked, and my lips trembled with the effort of controlling my emotions.

Perhaps I was making a mistake, after all.

'You've got no clothes for the Algarve,' said Lol, deftly attempting to put the lid upon my brilliant idea in one swift move.

I gritted my teeth. I'd thought about buying new clothes. Sundresses. Shorts. Stuff that let the sun in.

'Showing off all that skin! All the lumps and bumps!' Lol croaked, sounding more like my scornful mother than ever.

'Vitamin D,' I countered, gritting my teeth.

'You're being such a fool!' Lol rasped.

'Your legs'll swell in the heat! Think of your blood pressure! Needing the bathroom in the middle of the night! You won't know how to work the shower! And what if you don't like the food? What if you get ill?' Her voice got shriller and shriller, more like my mother's voice then ever, and then the final triumphant shout: 'What about me? You'll have to take me with you!'

'No way,' I thought.

There was going to be no little old lady on this trip.

I knew I could afford it, just about.

I knew that it would be an adventure, like no other I had ever had.

I knew that I would have a ball looking for new clothes to wear in a place I'd never been before.

I wanted this holiday so much. I'd take my chances.

So I booked it.

* * *

I'm sitting here, in the airport lounge, waiting for the flight to Faro to be called.

I'm wearing a flimsy, pretty, shoestring strappy dress with little sequined pumps.

My definitely-greying hair is streaked different shades of blonde and tied back in a cheeky little bunch.

I am so unlike the me of all the years leading up to this moment that I feel reborn – bright-eyed, cheerful and, yes, bubbly.

Definitely bubbly.

I'm going on the adventure of a lifetime.

There's me.

And, inside me, there's this little old lady.

She speaks with the voice of my mother and given half a chance she'd leap out and make my life a misery.

She can't wait to take over.

But it's not going to happen.

Me? Little old lady?

Well. Knickers to that...

THE END

© Irene Yates, 2013

17 Monday

18 Tuesday

19 Wednesday

20 Thursday

21 Friday

22 Saturday

23 Sunday

Making Your
Garden Grow

Got a few minutes to spare? Choose from Adrienne Wild's quick and easy summer jobs

If you only have...

5 Minutes

Move garden furniture around the lawn to stop the grass becoming too marked.

Stake taller flowering plants to prevent them from falling over. Shrubby twigs are brilliant for supporting plants and they're free and natural.

Pop bulbs of *Colchicum autumnale* on the windowsill indoors – you don't even need any soil for it to flower – and, after a couple of weeks, you'll get large pink/purple blooms sprouting. Plant it in the garden after flowering.

Sow parsley in the open ground or in pots to produce leaves for picking during the autumn.

Feed tomatoes with a high potash fertiliser. When small tomatoes have developed on the fourth truss, remove the growing tip two leaves above this truss.

10 Minutes

Pick early-ripening apples like 'George Clave' and eat straight from the tree, as they don't keep. If the fruit tastes sharp, leave the rest on the tree for a while longer.

Water, feed and deadhead to ensure a continued display of summer flowers in pots and borders.

15 Minutes

Plant some autumn-flowering bulbs, such as colchicums, *Nerine bowdenii* and autumn crocuses.

20 Minutes

Kill weeds that nestle among your paving using a weed knife or, for quick and easy results, spray with Weedol 2 – a fast-acting weedkiller that comes in pre-measured sachets.

30 Minutes

Cut back perennial shoots that are overhanging the lawn and replace any worn edges.

Remove blanket weed from the pond with a garden cane. Keep fish happy and healthy by oxygenating the water: either spray a jet of water over the pond for 10 minutes each day, or install a fountain.

24 Monday

25 Tuesday

26 Wednesday

27 Thursday

28 Friday

29 Saturday

30 Sunday

SEPTEMBER

31 Monday SUMMER BANK HOLIDAY

1 Tuesday

2 Wednesday

3 Thursday

4 Friday

5 Saturday

6 Sunday

Beef, Stilton & Ale Pie

Serves 4
Calories: 729
Fat: 42g
Saturated fat: 18g
Suitable for freezing: Filling only

* **250g ready-made puff pastry (half a packet of Jus-Rol All-Butter Puff pastry)**
* **Beaten egg, to glaze**

FOR THE FILLING:
* **3 tablespoons plain flour, seasoned**
* **600g (1¼lb) braising steak (chuck steak or shin of beef), cut into large cubes**
* **2 tablespoons vegetable oil**
* **2 medium onions, peeled and cut into wedges**
* **2 cloves garlic, peeled and chopped**
* **300ml (½ pint) stout (we used Guinness)**
* **150ml (¼ pint) hot beef stock**
* **1 teaspoon brown sugar**
* **1 bay leaf**
* **100g (3½oz) Stilton**

* *900ml-1.25 litre (1½-2 pint) capacity pudding bowl or pie dish*

1 To make the filling: Put the seasoned flour in a large bowl or bag. Add the beef and coat it well. Heat 1 tablespoon oil in a large pan and cook the beef in 2 batches for 3-4 minutes, until browned all over. Transfer it to a casserole dish. Set the oven to Gas Mark 3 or 160°C.

2 Add the onion and garlic and another tablespoon of the oil to the pan and cook them for 5 minutes until softened.

3 Pour in the stout and stock. Bring to the boil and add the sugar and bay leaf. Stir, then pour over the meat. Cover and cook in the oven for 1½ hours. Take out and leave to cool, if you have time.

4 Set the oven to Gas Mark 6 or 200°C. Roll out the pastry on a lightly-floured surface to at least 5cm (2in) larger than the top of the bowl. Cut out a round, then score it. Spoon the meat mixture into the bowl and add pieces of Stilton. Wet around the top of the dish, place a collar of pastry around it, made from trimmings, and then put on the lid. Seal the edges well, tuck the excess pastry under the rim. Brush with beaten egg. Place on a baking sheet, below the centre of the oven, and bake for 45-50 minutes, until the pastry is golden.

POST – CARD

Reader Karen Mossman, from Stretford, Manchester, nominates Aberystwyth in Wales

'Generations of my family have holidayed in Aberystwyth – I love looking at our old photos of grandparents and aunties and uncles walking down the prom, just as I have done with my own children. It's still delightfully old-fashioned, with its bandstand, pier and long promenade that bring back so many memories.'

7 Monday

8 Tuesday

9 Wednesday

10 Thursday

11 Friday

12 Saturday

13 Sunday

Fine Vintage

Dress up your boudoir in timeless style with this exquisite, gossamer-like throw

- Easy-peasy
- A Bit More Tricky
- **Hard-ish**
- Quite A Challenge

MEASUREMENTS

102 x 187cm/40 x 73½in, excluding edging.

MATERIALS

8 x 25g balls of Rico Design Fashion Romance (50% acrylic, 30% mohair, 20% wool) in Iced Blue (004). Size 4.50 crochet hook. You can buy the yarn online at womansweeklyshop.com/yarn or call 0800 024 1212.

TENSION

Each square to measure 17 x 17cm (when pinned out and blocked), using 4.50 hook.

ABBREVIATIONS

Ch, chain; **sp**, space; **dc**, double crochet; **st**, stitch; **tr**, treble; **htr**, half treble; **ttr**, triple treble; **yoh**, yarn over hook; **dtr3tog**, * wind yarn twice round hook, insert hook in place named, yoh and pull through, [yoh and pull through 2 loops on hook] twice, repeat from * twice more, yoh and pull through all 4 loops on hook; **ttr4tog**, * wind yarn 3 times round hook, insert hook in place named, yoh and pull through, [yoh and pull through 2 loops on hook] 3 times, repeat from * 3 times more, yoh and pull through all 5 loops on hook; **slst**, slip stitch.

NOTE

Yarn amounts are based on average requirements and are therefore approximate. Instructions in square brackets are worked as stated after 2nd bracket.

CABLE PANEL

First square: With 4.50 hook, make 6ch and join with a slst to form a ring.

1st round: 3ch (counts as 1tr), work 23tr in ring, slst in top of 3ch – 24 sts.

2nd round: 5ch (counts as 1ttr), miss st at base of 5ch, * wind yarn 3 times round hook, insert hook in next tr, yoh and pull through, [yoh and pull through 2 loops on hook] 3 times, repeat from * twice more, yoh and pull through all 4 loops on hook (ttr4tog made), 7ch, *** wind yarn 3 times round hook, insert hook in base of last st worked, yoh and pull through, [yoh and pull through 2 loops on hook] 3 times, ** wind yarn 3 times round hook, insert hook in next tr, yoh and pull through, [yoh and pull through 2 loops on hook] 3 times, repeat from ** twice more, yoh and pull through 5 loops on hook, 7ch ***, work from *** to ***, 6 times more working last ttr of last ttr4tog in missed st at beginning of round, slst in top of first ttr4tog – 8 petals made.

3rd round: 1ch (does not count as a st), 1dc in top of first ttr4tog, * [3ch, 1dc] 3 times in next 7chsp, 3ch, 1dc in top of next ttr4tog, repeat from *, ending last repeat with slst in first dc at beginning of round – thirty two 3chsp. **4th and 5th rounds:** Slst to centre of first 3chsp, 1ch (does not count as a st), 1dc in same 3chsp as slst, [3ch, 1dc in next 3chsp] 31 times, 3ch, slst in first dc at beginning of round. **6th round:** Slst to centre of first 3chsp, 1ch (does not count as a st), 1dc in same 3chsp as slst, * [3ch, 1dc in next 3chsp] 4 times, 3ch, miss next 3chsp, [dtr3tog, 5ch, ttr4tog, 4ch, slst in top of ttr4tog (a corner picot made), 5ch, dtr3tog] all in next 3chsp, 3ch, miss next 3chsp, 1dc in next 3chsp, repeat from * 3 times more, ending last repeat with slst in first dc at beginning of round. Fasten off.

Second square: Work 1st to 5th rounds of first square.

6th joining round: Slst to centre of first 3chsp, 1ch (does not count as a st), 1dc in same 3chsp as slst, * [3ch, 1dc in next 3chsp] 4 times, 3ch, miss next 3chsp, [dtr3tog, 5ch, ttr4tog] all in next 3chsp, 2ch, slst in base of 4ch (a corner picot made), 5ch, dtr3tog] all in next 3chsp, 3ch, miss next 3chsp, 1dc in next 3chsp, repeat from * once more, [3ch, 1dc in next 3chsp] 4 times, 3ch, miss next 3chsp, [dtr3tog, 5ch, ttr4tog] all in next 3chsp, 2ch, slst in corner picot on previous square, 1ch, slst in top of ttr4tog on current square, 2ch, slst in 3rd of next 5ch on previous square, 2ch, dtr3tog in same 3chsp as last ttr4tog worked,

1ch, slst in next 3chsp on previous square, 1ch, miss next 3chsp on current square, 1dc in next 3chsp on current square, [1ch, slst in next 3chsp on previous square, 1ch, 1dc in next 3chsp on current square] 4 times, 1ch, slst in next 3chsp on previous square, 1ch, miss next 3chsp on current square, dtr3tog in next 3chsp on current square, 2ch, slst in 3rd of next 5ch on previous square, 2ch, ttr4tog in same 3chsp as last dtr3tog worked, 2ch, slst in corner picot on previous square, 1ch, slst in top of ttr4tog of current square, 5ch, dtr3tog in same 3chsp as last ttr4tog, 3ch, miss next 3chsp on current square, slst in first dc at beginning of round. Fasten off. Make and join another 4 squares as before, to complete the first strip.

SECOND STRIP

Seventh square: Work 1st to 5th rounds of first square.

6th joining round: Join to side of sixth square and work as 6th round of first strip. Continue making and joining the second strip as follows:

Eighth square: Work 1st to 5th rounds of first square.

6th joining round: Slst to centre of first 3chsp, 1ch (does not count as a st), 1dc in same 3chsp as slst, [3ch, 1dc in next 3chsp] 4 times, 3ch, miss next 3chsp, [dtr3tog, 5ch, ttr4tog] all in next 3chsp, 2ch, slst in free corner picot at lower edge on previous square, 1ch, slst in top of ttr4tog on current square, 2ch, slst in 3rd of next 5ch on previous square, 2ch, dtr3tog in same 3chsp as last ttr4tog worked, 1ch, slst in next 3chsp on previous square, 1ch, miss next 3chsp on current square, 1dc in next 3chsp of current square, [1ch, slst in next 3chsp on previous square, 1ch, 1dc in next 3chsp on current square] 4 times, 1ch, slst in next 3chsp on previous square, 1ch, miss next 3chsp on current square, dtr3tog in next 3chsp on current square, 2ch, slst in 3rd of next 5ch on previous square, 2ch, ttr4tog in same 3chsp as last dtr3tog worked, 2ch, slst in corner picot joint, 1ch, slst in top of ttr4tog of current square, 2ch, slst in 3rd of next 5ch on fifth square, 2ch, dtr3tog in same 3chsp as last ttr4tog worked, 1ch, slst in next 3chsp on

fifth square, 1ch, miss next 3chsp on current square, 1dc in next 3chsp on current square, [1ch, slst in next 3chsp on fifth square, 1ch, 1dc in next 3chsp on current square] 4 times, 1ch, slst in next 3chsp on fifth square, 1ch, miss next 3chsp on current square, dtr3tog in next 3chsp on current square, 2ch, slst in 3rd of next 5ch on fifth square, 2ch, ttr4tog in same 3chsp as last dtr3tog worked, 2ch, slst in corner picot joint, 1ch, slst in top of ttr4tog of current square, 5ch, dtr3tog in same 3chsp as last ttr4tog worked, complete current square thus: 3ch, miss next 3chsp, 1dc in next 3chsp, [3ch, 1dc in next 3chsp] 4 times, 3ch, miss next 3chsp, [dtr3tog, 5ch, ttr4tog, 4ch, slst in top of ttr4tog, 5ch, dtr3tog] all in next 3chsp, 3ch, miss next 3chsp, slst in first dc at beginning of round. Fasten off.

Make and join another 4 squares to complete the second strip.

Now continue as before and join another 9 strips, making 66 squares in total.

EDGING

1st round: With right side facing and using 4.50 hook, rejoin yarn to side edge of throw to corner picots joint, 1ch (does not count as a st), 1dc at base of ch,* 3ch, then 1dc, 3ch, 1dc all in next 5chsp, [3ch, 1dc in next 3chsp] 6 times, then 1dc, 3ch, 1dc all in next 5chsp, 3ch, 1dc in corner picots joint, repeat from * to end, working 1dc, 3ch, 1dc all in free picots at each corner, ending last repeat with slst in first dc at beginning of round. **2nd round:** Slst in first 3chsp, [3ch, 1dc in next 3chsp] to end, working 1dc, 3ch, 1dc all in each corner 3chsp, ending last repeat with slst in first dc at beginning of round. **3rd round:** 1ch (does not count as a st), [1dc, 1htr, 1tr, 1htr, 1dc all in next 3chsp] to end, working 1dc 1htr, 3tr, 1htr, 1dc all in each corner 3chsp, ending last repeat with slst in first dc at beginning of round. Fasten off.

TO COMPLETE

Neaten loose ends, then pin out throw along outer edges to specified measurements. Cover with damp cloths and leave until cloths are dry.

Your Good Health

Ask Dr Mel

Q I really dread the winter – it's only September and I'm already feeling miserable. Could I have seasonal affective disorder?

A Seasonal affective disorder (SAD) is linked to low light levels, which can affect brain levels of melatonin and serotonin (sleep and mood-boosting chemicals), and natural body rhythms. It tends to start in the autumn (so feeling this way in September isn't unusual) and improve in the spring, and produces depression-type symptoms, like low mood and energy levels, and lack of interest in normal activities.

SAD may be severe enough to need treatment with antidepressants or talking treatments such as cognitive behavioural therapy. Sufferers are also advised to spend as much time as possible outside or near a window during winter, or to try light therapy. You can get an information pack from The Seasonal Affective Disorder Association, PO Box 989, Steyning BN44 3HG, or visit sada.org.uk.

But US researchers now say that SAD may not be as common as we thought, and that many people may feel worse in the winter simply because we're cooped up and less active. So it's worth seeing whether taking more exercise and joining in more social activities would help you; if not, I'd suggest discussing this with your GP.

TAKE 5...
Ways To Protect Your Eyes

1 HAVE AN EYE TEST every two years, and yearly after the age of 70 or if you have an eye condition. You may be entitled to free checks.

2 WEAR WRAPAROUND SUNGLASSES to reduce ultraviolet light exposure (look for the CE standard label when you buy them).

3 EAT a healthy, balanced diet containing a rainbow selection of fruit and veg, nuts, seeds and oily fish.

4 WEAR EYE protection for risky sports, DIY and gardening jobs.

5 DON'T SMOKE – for help to stop smoking, visit quit.org.uk.

A Great Exercise To...
Strengthen legs, bottom and hips

Mountain Climber

Start on the floor, on your tummy. Raise yourself up so your arms are straight, your legs stretched out straight behind you, resting on your toes. Your hands should be under your chest, just over shoulder-width apart. Bend your right knee and bring it up towards your right hand. Return and repeat with the left leg. Do 10 reps in all and build up to 20. *Well done!*

HOW THE EXPERTS STAY HEALTHY
Louise Hampton, chiropractor

What's in your medicine cabinet?
Paracetamol for pain and temperatures; Biofreeze Gel for injuries; Dioralyte for rehydrating myself and the kids after a tummy upset.

What's good in your fridge?
Eggs: versatile and so good for you; peppers and tomatoes, as they add colour to food.

What's your favourite exercise?
I run when I can, usually a couple of times a week. I also do some simple stretches every night to keep my spine healthy.

What's a special treat?
Dark chocolate. I love the taste and it's not too bad for me either…in small quantities, obviously.

If you can't sleep, what works?
Writing down everything I have to do lets me relax.

Any childhood remedy you still use?
Vicks VapoRub on the bottom of the feet to help stop coughing. It hasn't been scientifically proven, but I'm sure it helps!

● Download the British Chiropractic Association's stretches and exercises from chiropractic-uk.co.uk

14 Monday

15 Tuesday

16 Wednesday

17 Thursday

18 Friday

19 Saturday

20 Sunday

Easy Art
No Painting Required!

Create these lovely framed pictures using papers in autumn's rich colours

Apple Duo

1 Cut out two pieces of white paper or card, to the same size as the back of your frames.

2 Select your papers, ensuring you have two of each design. Then, using the apple template (below right), cut out nine pairs of red apples and nine pairs of green. To ensure the pairs look the same, cut the apples out from two sheets of matching wrapping paper. Roughly cut out your chosen section of paper together, then hold them firmly while cutting carefully around the template.

3 For each picture, stick the backs of nine apples evenly in position on to the white backgrounds using a glue stick, following our picture (left).

4 To create the 3D effect, stick a 1mm piece of double-sided tape, or a line of PVA glue, along the centre of each apple. Cut a length of string the height of the apple plus approximately 1cm for a stalk. Stick the string down the centre of the apple with the stalk protruding above the top.

5 Cut a 3mm-wide piece of double-sided tape and stick along the string. Fold a matching top apple in half, lengthways, and position on top of the string, pressing firmly. Open out the top apple. Repeat for all 18 apples.

6 Once dry, place in a box frame, or a frame with no glass, without using a mount.

● Papers from a selection at Paperchase (020 7467 6200; paperchase.co.uk). Ribba picture frame, 25cm wide x 25cm high, from a selection at Ikea (0845 355 1141; ikea.com). Bakelite clock; vintage snap game; set of four tins, all from a selection at Dotcomgiftshop (020 8746 2473; dotcomgiftshop.com).

You will need

- White paper or card
- Two frames
- Wrapping paper
- Glue stick
- Double-sided tape or PVA glue
- String

Falling Leaves

3 Glue 14 single leaves in position. Then, to create the 3D effect, fold a leaf in half lengthways and attach to the matching leaf on the picture with a thin piece of double-sided tape or a line of PVA glue along the crease. Press the top leaf firmly in position, then carefully open the leaf out. Repeat this process for all the leaves.

4 Once dry, place in a box frame, or a frame with no glass, ensuring your design is placed evenly within the mount (see our picture, left, for guidance).

● *Light Oak Sticky-Backed Plastic, from a selection at Homebase (0845 077 8888; homebase.co.uk). Papers, from a selection at Paperchase (020 7467 6200; paperchase.co.uk). Similar white box frame with mount, from a selection at Frame Company (0844 800 9958; frame-company.co.uk). Walnut owl, from a selection at Howkapow (0117 942 4000; howkapow.com).*

You will need

- ✿ Oak-effect sticky-backed plastic
- ✿ Tracing paper
- ✿ Wrapping paper
- ✿ White paper or card
- ✿ Double-sided tape or PVA glue
- ✿ Box frame or glassless frame

pair firmly together while cutting around the template.

2 Cut a piece of white paper or card to fit the back of your frame. Then, using our picture as a guide, peel off the backing from the trunk and stick the tree to the white background.

Enlarge tree template on a photocopier by 400%

1 Enlarge the tree template (right) on a photocopier by 400% and cut out the shape from the oak-effect sticky-backed plastic. Trace off the leaf template and cut out 14 pairs of leaves from the wrapping paper.

TIP To ensure the pairs of leaves look the same, cut out from two sheets of matching wrapping paper. Start by roughly cutting out your chosen pairs, then hold each

TAKING A CHANCE
On Love

Mike Love was gorgeous. And I believed every word that he said. Regardless of whatever everyone else thought...

Mike Love. Everyone warned me about him, but I didn't listen. Then he turned out exactly as they predicted.

I never really noticed him until the fourth form. Then – forgive the cliché – it was love at first sight. I should never have confided in Anna, my best friend, though.

'Mike Love?' she said, her eyebrows disappearing behind her fringe. 'You've really lost it this time, Geri.'

'What do you mean? He's all right.'

Anna made a grunting noise. 'He's a dreamer. Yesterday he forgot all his books, the day before that his jumper was inside out. And last week...' Anna began to giggle '...he spent a whole morning with *If I Had A Brain I'd Be Dangerous* on a sign that Nicky Pierce had taped to his back.'

She broke up laughing. Most of the time we would giggle at stuff like that together. But not this time.

'That's not funny,' I said.

'Ah, I get it,' Anna replied. 'You want to go out with him because you feel sorry for him.'

But I didn't. I wanted to go out with Mike because he was gorgeous. He had this curly mop of hair just begging for a hand to run through it, deep sea-blue eyes you could drown in from half a playground away, and a smile that demanded you match it with one in return. And when we went out for our first date – a milkshake at Barry's Burgers in town – we just clicked.

'I'm going to start my own business when I leave school,' Mike said, nodding towards Barry flipping burgers. 'Start a business and become a millionaire.'

'That's fantastic,' I said. My eyes must have blazed with admiration over the top of my milkshake. 'What will you do?'

'I'm not sure yet. I just know I'm destined to be rich.'

I believed him. As we went from fourth form to fifth form to sixth, as I stayed on at school and Mike left, I believed every word he said. Regardless of whatever anyone else thought.

'Engaged?' Dad looked stunned; Mum stood beside him open-mouthed. 'You and Mike are engaged?'

'Getting engaged,' I explained. 'Actually, Mike wanted to do it all properly and ask your permission.'

'But..?'

'But he lost his nerve.' I paused. 'It doesn't matter, does it?'

'Well, no,' Mum said. 'It doesn't matter. It's just...well...' Her eyes flicked towards Dad and then back to me. 'Are you sure you want to marry Mike?'

'I'm sure.'

I could see Dad struggling to find an argument against my decision. The trouble was everyone liked Mike. He just gave them all the impression he would never amount to much.

'What about his prospects?' Dad said at last. 'He works in Barry's Burgers. Do you really want to spend your life with a man who cooks burgers for a living?'

I grinned, glad Dad had brought that up. 'He's going to start his own business when we're married. We're going to be rich.'

Dad sighed. 'And what if you don't become rich?'

'I don't know,' I said with a carefree shrug. 'Things will turn out all right in the end.'

Mum and Dad exchanged another look. A silent message passed between them which I never understood when I was nineteen. Now, with children and grandchildren of my own, I've a good idea.

We've got to let her make her own mistakes.

So Dad smiled and gave me a hug. 'And I sincerely hope you do become rich.'

When Mum joined him, she added, 'And I hope you're happy. Who knows what the future will bring? If you love each other sometimes that's enough.'

Over the years that followed I could never fault Mike for trying. He opened his first burger bar when he was twenty-two. By the time he was twenty-four it had

> '*He's a dreamer, head in the clouds*'

almost bankrupted us. Then he started a window-cleaning round. The plan was to build up to doing offices and factories and flats. Until Mike discovered he was scared of heights.

But it's funny. At certain moments your life can completely change direction. It happened for us when Mike came home from work after another attack of vertigo.

'I'm pregnant,' I said.

Mike's mouth fell open. 'That's...that's...'

'Wonderful?'

'Yes,' he said. 'Wonderful. But we don't have any money.'

'I know,' I replied. 'I'll have to leave college and...'

But now Mike was frowning.

'What is it?'

And then he had the best idea of his life.

I lifted the knife and Mike's hand closed over mine. Together we raised it to the large *40th* iced on top of our anniversary cake. As we cut into it we were dazzled by the flashes from everyone's cameras – our parents, children, and grandchildren.

'It seems I wasn't taking a chance at all,' I whispered.

Mike frowned. 'What do you mean?'

'It doesn't matter,' I said, kissing his wonderful confused face. 'Not a bit.'

When Mike started his businesses I should have got more involved. The trouble is until you've tried something you don't know if you'll be any good at it.

After Andrew was born my children's-furniture business took off in a big way. We may not be millionaires but we've done well. And with children and grandchildren like ours, we're rich anyway.

Because Mike found out what he was good at, too. Everything from messy play at the toddler groups to arts and crafts at the school fair, from cooking and cleaning to even helping with their homework. Mike was no businessman, and I still sometimes find him daydreaming with his head in the clouds. But it doesn't matter. Things turned out all right in the end.

THE END
© *Geoff Bagwell, 2013*

21 Monday

22 Tuesday

23 Wednesday

24 Thursday

25 Friday

26 Saturday

27 Sunday

Krisskross

All you have to do is fit these words into the grid, reading across and down.

3 LETTERS
UAE
USA

6 LETTERS
POLAND
SWEDEN

9 LETTERS
AUSTRALIA
SINGAPORE
VENEZUELA

10 LETTERS
LUXEMBOURG
MADAGASCAR

Wordsearch 2

L	H	C	H	E	E	S	E	S	W
E	C	C	R	C	P	N	C	A	A
M	I	H	I	S	A	O	R	U	L
O	I	P	I	W	T	K	A	S	S
N	D	R	K	C	D	N	E	A	E
A	C	A	H	R	K	N	T	G	L
D	U	E	L	R	O	E	A	E	O
E	G	E	T	A	P	P	N	S	C
G	D	R	U	M	S	T	I	C	K
I	E	T	A	L	O	C	O	H	C

Find all the food listed below in the grid except one – they run either forwards or backwards, horizontally, vertically or diagonally, but always in a straight unbroken line. The missing word is your answer.

CAKE	PATE
CHEESE	PORK PIE
CHICKEN	SALAD
CHOCOLATE	SANDWICH
COLESLAW	SAUSAGE
CRISPS	SCONE
DRUMSTICK	SCOTCH EGG
LEMONADE	TEA

Solutions to this month's puzzle on November puzzles

SOLUTIONS FOR AUGUST 2015

QUICK CROSSWORD
ACROSS 1 Tapestry **5** Pips **9** Roomy **10** Idolise **11** Balm **12** Lecterns **14** Barked
15 Sadden **18** Put-you-up **20** Defy **23** Illicit **24** Snide **25** Etna **26** Enlarged
DOWN 1 Throb **2** Prowler **3** Stye **4** Rained **6** Icier **7** Stetson **8** Postman
13 Rejoice **14** Baptise **16** Dieting **17** Mutton **19** Talon **21** Yield **22** Asia

Answer: MAGNOLIA

28 Monday

29 Tuesday

30 Wednesday

1 Thursday

2 Friday

3 Saturday

4 Sunday

OCTOBER

5 Monday

6 Tuesday

7 Wednesday

8 Thursday

9 Friday

10 Saturday

11 Sunday

Take a...
Tea Towel
...and transform it into a truly delightful home accessory

Teacake Tea Cosy

The very apt image of the Tunnocks Tea Cake on this fun tea towel is the perfect size for a standard tea cosy to fit a four-cup teapot. All you need is one or two matching tea towels, lining fabric and wadding.

1 Measure the height and circumference of your teapot. Using these measurements, cut out a cosy-shaped paper pattern, adding a 1cm seam allowance all around.

2 Using your paper pattern, cut two pieces from your tea towels, two from your chosen lining fabric and two from the wadding.

3 For the loop, cut a 10 x 3.5cm piece from the tea-towel remnants. Press the long edges in by 5mm on both sides then fold in half lengthways with raw edges inside. Machine-stitch together 2mm in from the open edge.

4 Fold in half to create a loop and position on the right side of the tea cosy at the centre top, looped end facing down. Tack in place.

5 Taking a 1cm seam allowance, machine-stitch the outer cosy pieces, right sides together, leaving the bottom edge open.

6 Place a wadding piece behind the wrong side of each lining piece and tack in place. Join the two lining pieces right sides together and machine-stitch around the 1cm seam allowance. Trim the seam and snip into the curve to help the dome have a smooth shape. Repeat on the outer pieces.

7 Place the outer tea cosy into the inside of the lining, so the right sides of the lining and main tea cosy fabric are facing each other.

8 Machine-stitch the bottom edges together leaving a 6cm gap. Pull the tea cosy through the gap to the right side and hand-sew the opening closed.

● Tunnocks Tea Towel, from a selection at Gillian Kyle (0141 248 8702; gilliankyle.com). Radio, from a selection at Dotcomgiftshop (020 8746 2473; dotcomgiftshop.com). Mugs, from a selection at Howkapow (0117 942 4000; howkapow.com). Milk jug, from a selection at We Love Kaoru (welovekaoru.com).

Feature: Dilly Orme. Styling: Emily Dawe. Photos: Sussie Bell

Handy Tote Bag

Pretty Cushion Pad

Make cushion pads out of two matching tea towels – it's a great way of co-ordinating your kitchen soft furnishings.

1 Use your cushion pad to make two templates. For the front, draw around the pad adding the depth of the pad, plus a 1.5cm seam allowance. Cut out one front pad piece from one tea towel using the template.

2 For the back, draw around the pad, adding a 1.5cm seam allowance, then cut the template in half across the width, so you now have two pieces. Add 8cm to one piece to form the envelope back, piece A. Add 2cm to the other half, piece B.

3 From a second tea towel, cut out one size A piece and one size B piece.

4 Neaten the envelope back edges by folding in 1 x 1cm and machine-stitch in place. Lay the two back pieces over each other to form the opening for the pad, tack and pin in place.

5 Using the largest length stitch on a sewing machine, sew a line of stitching round any corners of the pad top piece. Draw the thread up slightly to gather excess fabric so it will fall softly over the curve of the pad.

6 Cut two lengths of webbing 80cm long, fold in half and place on the right side of the back piece in a position that will tie easily on to your chair. Sew in place within the seam allowance, so the long lengths are facing towards the main body of the cover.

7 Machine-stitch the front and back pieces right sides together leaving a small gap for turning through – use pins and tack first if necessary. Use small scissors to snip into the curves to ensure a smooth finish. Turn through and press, place your pad into the cover and hand-stitch the opening closed.

● *Blue Vinegar Pots Tea Towel, from a selection at Linen Prints (07870 193038; linenprints.co.uk).*

One tea towel and a length of pretty lace ribbon is all you need to create this bag – ideal for storage.

1 Take a 1.5cm seam allowance throughout.

2 Fold your tea towel in half, so the short ends meet, right sides together.

3 Machine-stitch the two ends of the tea towel together.

4 Fold and press the tea towel, so the seam forms the centre of the back of the bag. Sew across one end to form the bottom.

5 Cut two 52cm lengths of lace or webbing. Position the ends 3cm either side of the centre of the bag top and 3cm below the top edge.

6 Machine-stitch the lace in position in a box formation to give the handles strength.

7 Turn the bag through to the right side. Press, and trim away any excess threads.

● *Red Doodle Flower Tea Towel, from a selection at Jangneus (01865 988074; jangneus.com). Hook, from a selection at Dotcomgiftshop (020 8746 2473; dotcomgiftshop.com).*

POST – CARD

Reader Gloria Wilding, from Prescot, Merseyside, nominates Hornsea in Yorkshire

'Visiting Hornsea always brings back fond memories for me of childhood holidays in the 1950s. Don't miss the Mere, Hornsea's wonderful expanse of water, with its swan island, café and lots of wildlife to see in a tranquil setting. And I always enjoy the fascinating Hornsea Museum, containing a variety of examples from the old Hornsea Pottery, from which I've bought many lovely pieces over the years.'

12 Monday

13 Tuesday

14 Wednesday

15 Thursday

16 Friday

17 Saturday

18 Sunday

Ginger Pumpkin
Biscuits

Makes 12	
Calories per biscuit: 235	
Fat: 6g	
Saturated fat: 2g	
Suitable for freezing: ✔	

* 2 tablespoons runny honey
* 30g (1oz) unsalted butter
* 60g (2oz) light muscovado sugar
* 250g (8oz) self-raising flour
* 1 teaspoon ground ginger
* Finely grated zest of 1 orange
* 60g (2oz) ground almonds
* 1 large egg, beaten
* 2-4 tablespoons orange juice

TO DECORATE:
* 250g packet ready-to-roll icing
* 2 teaspoons runny honey
* 1 apple
* Egg yellow and scarlet food paste colouring

* 7.5cm (3in) round, fluted cutter
* 2 baking sheets, lined with baking parchment
* 5cm (2in) biscuit cutter

1 Put the honey, butter and sugar into a small pan and stir over a low heat until the butter is melted.

2 Sieve the flour and ginger into a bowl. Add the orange zest and ground almonds.

3 Pour in the egg, melted butter mixture and orange juice into the dry ingredients. Stir with a wooden spoon until the mixture comes together.

4 Knead the mixture on a lightly floured surface for a couple of minutes, then wrap in cling film and pop in the freezer for 30 minutes to firm up.

5 Set the oven to Gas Mark 4 or 180°C. Roll out the dough on a parchment-lined surface, to a 5mm (¼in) thickness and stamp out the biscuit shapes, using the fluted cutter.

6 Put the biscuits on to the lined baking sheets. Bake for 15-20 minutes until pale golden. Cool on a wire rack.

7 To decorate: Roll out the icing on baking parchment and stamp out rounds using the biscuit cutter. Brush the biscuit centres with honey and place the icing on top.

8 Cut one-third off the apple, avoiding the core. Carve out 2 eyes and a mouth on the apple flesh. Mix the food colourings to make orange and paint the cut side of the apple. Stamp on to the iced biscuits. Repeat with the other biscuits. Leave to dry. Store in an airtight container for up to 1 week.

Tip from our kitchen

To stop the icing sticking to the tabletop or rolling pin, put the block of icing into a plastic folder (the kind you use for paper) before you roll it.

Towards Equality

A woman's place was still in the home, but she could have more of a life outside it if she followed social convention. And we finally got the same voting rights as men

Things Husbands Hate

All he asks is that you should not throw bothers in his way

"IF you want to make your husband happy," said a very wise old wife, "don't keep on trying to please him ... just prevent yourself from displeasing him, and that will be enough. A man does not want to be amused and (male happy, like a child — all he asks is that you should not throw bothers in his way, and prevent him from enjoying the happiness which he is quite able to find for himself."

There's a great deal of truth in that, you know, and we don't always recognise it, we women, more's the pity. We make great efforts to astonish and delight our menfolk. But they don't want that— all they ask of us is just not to throw in their way the things they hate.

Now, what are the things that a man hates? First and foremost comes, I think :

A FUSS MADE BY ANYONE EXCEPT HIMSELF

QUITE a number of men are fussy over their own affairs, but few will admit that any woman has the right to copy him in this. They seem to take it for granted that women can do everything easily, quietly, without anxiety, or noise, or talk. As long as a woman can manage this, he likes to have her with him, but the moment she starts to cluck and flutter he "wishes her further."

A young man very much in love is often an exception to this rule. He has his own means of calming down a pretty girl's agitations, and enjoys using them. But when once he is married matters change— he then hates "all this sing-song over nothing" just as much as any other man.

A SCENE OF ANY KIND

GONE—I hope for good—are the days when a wife could screw anything that she liked out of her husband by means of ...

(caption under illustration) He hates "all this sing-song over nothing."

TOO MUCH TALK ABOUT DAILY BOTHERS

WHEN he comes back from the office, he doesn't start straight and tell you all about the row there was over those forgotten letters, and the nasty business with the new office hat, and the disagreeableness of the accountant about that open window, and the error which made it necessary to have all those accounts re-copied. No, he leaves business bothers behind him, and comes back to enjoy his few hours of rest and home-life. No sooner has the office door swung to behind him than he has shaken himself free of all the office "truck" and troubles.

And he expects his woman to do the same—shut off her domestic bothers and be ready to enjoy the evening or the Sunday with him. He doesn't understand how much harder it is for her. And there's nothing that he hates worse than to have his dinner, or his visit to the pictures, or his game of tennis spoiled by a long litany of miseries—the children, the servants, the tradesmen, the neighbours.

PECULIARITIES IN HIS WOMEN-FOLK

YOU may find one man in a thousand who, being rather original himself, likes his folk to be the same, and is pleased when his wife or sister or fiancée makes herself remarkable. But, as a rule, it is only the men who are not engaged to you and never mean to be who are delighted when your get-up makes everyone turn round and look after you, or when you express opinions which cause a whisper and a rustle to run through the room. But the once you really belong to simply hate it. They are red while it happens, and remember it afterwards in a way that keeps them wondering uneasily what fool trick you ...

He's just a big baby

But it was you who had to bite your tongue and not displease

In this article from 1922, we explained how 'a man does not want to be amused and made happy, all he asks is that you not throw bothers in his way. He may make a fuss over things that upset him, but the moment she 'starts to cluck…' Nor, once home from work, can he bear to hear about your domestic troubles. He wants you 'ready to enjoy the evening with him…hates to have his dinner, a visit to the pictures or his game of tennis spoiled by a long litany of miseries'. A contented life could be had simply by not displeasing your husband, even if he was a 'great, overgrown baby'. So that's that sorted then…

THE HEN-PECKING WIFE

It is the duty of every wife to spur her man onwards

YOU'D never think that anyone would write an article in praise of hen-pecking, would you? Somehow the henpecked husband always gets the pity of the average person.

"Poor chap! He does lead a life! His wife is always at him over something or other—a regular hen-pecker. It must be terrible to be tied to a woman like that!"

So we talk. And we rarely remember that some women have to be hen-peckers. For there are men who would never do anything worth while unless they had a woman to edge him on. Without provocation of some sort there are many people who would accomplish nothing. They must be stimulated by somebody.

It often happens that a girl who appeared quite meek turns into something of a shrew after marriage. "You'd never have thought that Violet would have become a henpecker," says someone who knew her well. But it's quite on the cards that Violet was forced into the hen-pecking rôle. Don't blame her until you know the facts.

Plenty of women marry without knowing the characters of their mates.

One of the truest things ever spoken is the oft-quoted saying that "one must live with a person to know them." Rarely is it that couples know each other during courtship. The knowledge they gain after marriage comes thick and fast. Sometimes it is beautiful knowledge, but sometimes it isn't.

A woman goes through a bitter moment when she realises that her man isn't all she thought him, that he lacks ambition, that his line is always the one of least resistance, and that he takes no thought for the morrow so long as they can muddle along through to-day.

WISE HEN-PECKING

IF a woman loves her man she isn't content to see him muddling. She wants him to do big things. She knows that he has the brain, the strength, and the capability for doing them, but he lacks the spur. And she sets herself to be the spur. And, in seeking to spur him forward, she appears as a henpecker. We say that she nags. But, if she told us what she thought, it might be that he'd never do anything unless she nagged. He has to be henpecked. It is true. There are men like that. But the mistake the wife makes is to keep on henpecking all the time. Just as constant dripping wears away a stone, so continual nagging wears a man out. Petty hen-pecking does not stimulate. It is of the unwise brand.

Then what about wise henpecking?

The world is full of men who owe the best in themselves and the things they have accomplished to the women who spurred them to effort. It is never a question of a wife holding the whip-hand. There is no driving in true marriage. But a woman can do much by suggestion and a wise insinuation. And she is quite right to use a little henpecking at the right times with the man who needs it.

'It is such a little thing to be happy'

Our pages were filled with advice reflecting the pressure wives felt to be perfect: on the one hand, nagging a little to bring out the best in your husband; on the other, being compliant enough to keep the peace

THAT LITTLE WORD "OBEY."

A little discussion about a much-talked-about question.

WHY should there be all this nonsensical talk about women obeying their husbands? Personally, I think all the trouble in this direction comes through the interference of, let us say, Mrs. Brown next door, who, when she sees little Mrs. Newlywed doing some little thing for her husband, says : "I wouldn't do that for my husband. I'd tell him straight I wouldn't.". I dare say Mrs. Brown is one of those miserable, ill-tempered ... have a moment ...

... he married ; the girl who said it would be a pleasure to sew on his buttons and to cook his dinners. This was a different sort of creature altogether.

A word or two from him in the matter of talking things over would probably have set the matter right, but he is too indignant, and probably says many things he wishes he had left unsaid. And so the trouble gets worse and the little rift widens, while all the time ...

A Man's Woman

THE woman who makes a man happiest in the world —the woman whom he loves longest and understands best—is the woman who loves him JUST ENOUGH.

Just enough to make him happy —and not enough to make him tired.

Just enough to flatter him— and not enough to make him conceited.

Just enough to appreciate his tastes—and not enough to coddle his whims.

Just enough to be glad when he's around—and not enough to be sad when he's away.

Just enough to inspire him in his work—and not enough to distract him from it.

... enough to be proud of him ...

19 Monday

20 Tuesday

21 Wednesday

22 Thursday

23 Friday

24 Saturday

25 Sunday

- Easy-peasy
- A Bit More Tricky
- **Hard-ish**
- Quite A Challenge

Yes, you really can knit a real wall clock – all you need to do is add the mechanism and you have a working, art deco-style timepiece

MEASUREMENTS
26.5 x 26.5cm/10½ x 10½in.

MATERIALS
1 x 50g (115m) ball of Rowan Cotton Glacé (100% cotton) in each of Oyster (730), Dawn Grey (831) and Bleached (726); 1 x 25g (100m) ball of Anchor Artiste Metallic (80% viscose, 20% metallised polyester) in Gold (00300). Pair of 3¼mm (No. 10) knitting needles. Piece of 26 x 26cm/10¼ x 10¼in stout card; clock-maker kit (find one at hobbycraft.co.uk). You can buy the yarn online at womansweeklyshop.com/yarn or call 0800 024 1212.

TENSION
23 stitches and 32 rows, to 10 x 10cm, over stocking stitch, using 3¼mm needles and Cotton Glacé yarn.

ABBREVIATIONS
K, knit; **p**, purl; **st**, stitch; **tog**, together; **ss**, stocking st (k on right side and p on wrong side); **yf**, yarn forward to make a st.

NOTE
Yarn amounts are based on average requirements and are therefore approximate.

BACK

With 3¼mm needles and Oyster, cast on 62 sts.

Beginning with a k row, ss 8 rows. Using separate small balls of yarn for each coloured area and twisting yarns together on wrong side at joins, work as follows:

9th row: K6 Oyster, 50 Bleached, 6 Oyster. **10th row:** P6 Oyster, 50 Bleached, 6 Oyster. **11th to 16th rows:** Repeat 9th and 10th rows, 3 times. **17th row:** K6 Oyster, 6 Bleached, 38 Dawn Grey, 6 Bleached, 6 Oyster. **18th row:** P6 Oyster, 6 Bleached, 38 Dawn Grey, 6 Bleached, 6 Oyster. **19th to 24th rows:** Repeat 17th and 18th rows, 3 times.

25th row: K6 Oyster, 6 Bleached, 6 Dawn Grey, 26 Oyster, 6 Dawn Grey, 6 Bleached, 6 Oyster. **26th row:** P6 Oyster, 6 Bleached, 6 Dawn Grey, 26 Oyster, 6 Dawn Grey, 6 Bleached, 6 Oyster. **27th to 32nd rows:** Repeat 25th and 26th rows, 3 times.

33rd row: K6 Oyster, 6 Bleached, 6 Dawn Grey, 6 Oyster, 14 Bleached, 6 Oyster, 6 Dawn Grey, 6 Bleached, 6 Oyster. **34th row:** P6 Oyster, 6 Bleached, 6 Dawn Grey, 6 Oyster, 14 Bleached, 6 Oyster, 6 Dawn Grey, 6 Bleached, 6 Oyster. **35th to 42nd rows:** Repeat 33rd and 34th rows, 4 times. **43rd row:** K6 Oyster, 6 Bleached, 6 Dawn Grey, 6 Oyster, with Bleached, k7, yf, k2tog, k5, 6 Oyster, 6 Dawn Grey, 6 Bleached, 6 Oyster. **44th row:** As 34th row. **45th to 54th rows:** Repeat 33rd and 34th rows, 4 times. **55th and 62nd rows:** Repeat 25th and 26th rows, 4 times. **63rd to 70th rows:** Repeat 17th and 18th rows, 4 times. **71st to 78th rows:** Repeat 9th and 10th rows, 4 times. With Oyster, ss 7 rows. Cast off.

FRONT

With 3¼mm needles and Oyster, cast on 62 sts.

Using separate small balls of yarn for each coloured area and twisting yarns together on wrong side at joins, work as follows:

1st row: K. **2nd row:** P. **3rd row:** K2 Oyster, 58 Dawn Grey, 2 Oyster. **4th row:** P2 Oyster, 58 Dawn Grey, 2 Oyster. **5th to 18th rows:** Repeat 3rd and 4th rows, 8 times. **19th row:** K2 Oyster, 13 Dawn Grey, 32 Oyster, 13 Dawn Grey, 2 Oyster.

20th row: P2 Oyster, 13 Dawn Grey, 32 Oyster, 13 Dawn Grey, 2 Oyster. **21st row:** As 19th row. **22nd row:** P2 Oyster, 13 Dawn Grey, 2 Oyster, 28 Bleached, 2 Oyster, 13 Dawn Grey, 2 Oyster. **23rd row:** K2 Oyster, 13 Dawn Grey, 2 Oyster, 28 Bleached, 2 Oyster, 13 Dawn Grey, 2 Oyster. **24th to 42nd rows:** Repeat 22nd and 23rd rows, 8 times, then work 22nd row again. **43rd row:** K2 Oyster, 13 Dawn Grey, 2 Oyster, with Bleached, k14, yf, k2tog, k12, 2 Oyster, 13 Dawn Grey, 2 Oyster.

44th to 63rd rows: Repeat 22nd and 23rd rows, 10 times. **64th row:** As 20th row. **65th and 66th rows:** As 19th and 20th rows. **67th to 82nd rows:** Repeat 3rd and 4th rows, 8 times. With Oyster, ss 3 rows. Cast off.

TO MAKE UP

Using Gold, Swiss-darn numbers and letters on front as shown on chart (below). Pin out front and back to measurements given, spray with cold water and leave until dry. Join back and front together along cast-on edge and row-end edges. Make a hole on stout card to match hole on front and back. Insert stout card and join cast-off edge. Using knitted front as clock face, attach mechanism as directed.

Insert the mechanism into the centre of the back of the clock

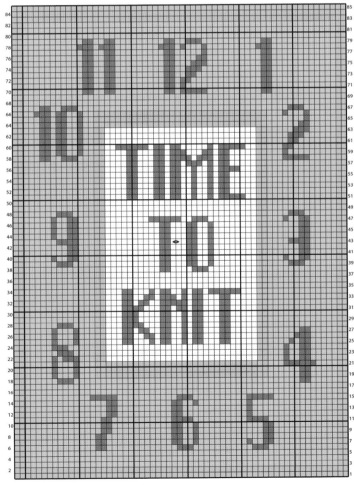

Heartbroken

Life hasn't been easy over the last few years. I'd never have got through it without the support of the best husband a woman could wish for

I've been thinking about you a lot recently. About how much I owe you, and how different my life would have been without you; and never more so than now.

Not everyone understands why I've been so keen to organise this thirtieth anniversary party. Why I've planned a big celebration in the poshest hotel in town and even booked a church for a 'renewal of wedding vows' service beforehand.

'Isn't this all a bit over the top, Cass?' my older sister Emmy asked as she helped me try on dresses. 'Gareth and I have been married for nearly forty years and you don't see me rushing to throw a party.'

Emmy always has been a bit of a glass-half-empty person, though. So I just smiled and humoured her.

'You know me,' I said. 'Always got to be the centre of attention.'

In fact, nothing could be further from the truth and, if anything, I can't help feeling I've been the centre of attention way too much over the years. So, it's not about the public display. It's about the fact that I truly want to celebrate my marriage, to give thanks for all the good things in life and just enjoy myself for a while.

I felt a bit sorry for Emmy that day. She looked somehow beaten, as she sat there in her fawn trouser suit, tucking a strand of greying hair behind her ear. She hasn't had the problems I've had, but she's never really seemed properly happy, either. But maybe you need to nearly lose everything before you can appreciate what you've got.

'Will I do?' I asked, as I paraded in front of her in the cerise dress I'd finally decided was the one. I loved the way it floated around me, not clinging to my body but allowing me freedom to move and to breathe.

'It's a bit bright,' she said, a tinge of disapproval in her voice.

But I didn't listen. I've got to live life to the full now. I owe you that much.

* * *

Fortunately, my daughter, Felicity, has been a bit more enthusiastic about the idea of the vow renewal and the big party.

'It's great that you and Dad want to do this,' she said, as she helped me pick out shoes. Well, she was supposed to be helping me pick out shoes, but actually she had five pairs lined up that she'd got an eye on for herself.

I was so glad she understood. Life hasn't been easy over the last few years and I have no idea if I'd have even made it through without the support of the best husband a woman could wish for. I've needed a lot of love and support and it's always been unfailingly there. If that isn't worth celebrating, I don't know what is.

'It's partly my way of saying thanks to

> *I loved the way it floated around me, not clinging to my body*

him,' I said, suddenly feeling the need to bite my lip to hold back tears as I fiddled with an ankle strap.

'Oh, Mum,' she said. 'Don't get upset. I know things have been rough, but this is your happy ending. You've both been through so much and now you need to let your hair down and relax.'

She was right, of course. Things were touch and go for a while, but luckily my marriage was strong, and my family helped me through. In the end, I was strong enough to survive; with your help, of course.

'I'll take these,' I said, twirling around the shoe shop in the sandals I just knew would go with the dress I'd already chosen.

'And I'll take these,' Felicity said, scooping up three assorted pairs of killer heels.

'Felicity!' I said. 'Think of your poor bank balance.'

'Don't worry,' she said. 'It's only money.

You only live once, so you might as well make the most of it.'

'Yes,' I thought. 'You only live once, but sometimes you need a second chance and I've been lucky enough to be given one.'

* * *

So now, I'm standing at the door of the church, preparing to walk up the aisle for the second time. Heading for the second chance I never thought I'd get and ready to welcome it with open arms.

I'm wearing the dress that Emmy didn't really approve of. 'It's a bit mutton dressed as lamb,' she'd said, when we got it home.

But to be honest, I don't care. I feel renewed, and if I want to celebrate by wearing a dress designed for a woman twenty years younger, then I will. I think you'd like that idea.

And, of course, I'm thinking about you again, about how much you've given me and how much I need to make sure I repay you by grasping every opportunity. Life is precious and I'm going to drink in every minute of it with my new-found unquenchable thirst.

But as the organ begins to play, I know I must stop thinking of you now and focus on my husband instead. I can see the back of his head, so familiar and dear to me. And then he turns and smiles and I feel my heart soar.

I never knew much about you, as it happens. Only that you died far too young, in an accident, and that your death gave me the chance to live. Because, before you came into my life, my heart was literally broken. And without your gift, and the bravery of your family who agreed to the transplant, I might not even be here.

So, as I walk up the aisle to renew my vows with my husband of thirty years, I just want to say thank you, again. Because I know, with every beat of my heart, that I owe you everything.

THE END
© *Helen M. Hunt, 2013*

26 Monday

27 Tuesday

28 Wednesday

29 Thursday

30 Friday

31 Saturday

1 Sunday

Making Your
Garden Grow

Got a few minutes (or an hour) to spare? Choose from Adrienne Wild's get-ready-for-winter jobs

If you only have...

5 Minutes

Sow parsley to provide plenty of leaves for winter and spring use. This herb is rich in vitamins A, B, C and iron, and chewing the leaves is the best way to eliminate bad breath!

10 Minutes

Sow winter-ready 'Meteor' peas for an early crop.

Take 5-7cm cuttings from perennial bedding plants (pelargoniums, fuchsias). Root them on a shaded windowsill under a polythene tent.

20 Minutes

30 Minutes

Dig up, divide and replant congested clumps of herbaceous perennials.

Rake out dead grass in the lawn.

45 Minutes

Dig up and divide large clumps of herbaceous perennials that are more than three years old. Discard old woody parts of the plants, such as the crown, and split up the younger outer parts into smaller pieces.

Lift maincrop potatoes and store in sacks for winter.

Plant out spring cabbage seedlings; cover in cloches.

60 Minutes

Tart up a tatty lawn with spring bulbs, such as Snake's head fritillaries.

Loosen compacted gravel areas and top up levels to avoid drainage problems in the winter.

Clip your beech hedge now and the leaves will remain on the plant for the winter. Use secateurs to cut back wayward shoots. Make sure you shred the trimmings before putting them in the compost bin.

NOVEMBER

Bow Belles

You'll turn heads with these knitted accessories – they're touchy-feely, too!

MEASUREMENTS

Hat: Fits average woman's head.
Bag: Approximately 18cm/7in high and 24cm/9½in wide at top edge.

MATERIALS

Hat: 2 x 50g (240m) balls of Rico Design Creative Reflection (46% wool, 46% acrylic, 8% polyester) in Beige (002).
Bag: 4 x 50g (240m) balls of Rico Design Creative Reflection (46% wool, 46% acrylic, 8% polyester) in Red (003) and 1 ball in Dark Grey (006); 24 x 15cm piece of millinery blocking net or stout card.
Both items: Pair of 3¾mm (No. 9) and 4mm (No. 8) knitting needles. The yarn can be purchased from Black Sheep Wools, call 01925 764231 or visit blacksheep.com

TENSION

Hat: 22 stitches and 29 rows, to 10 x 10cm, over stocking stitch, using 4mm needles and two strands of yarn together. **Bag:** 20 stitches and 28 rows, to 10 x 10cm, over stocking stitch, using 4mm needles and three strands of yarn together.

ABBREVIATIONS

K, knit; **p**, purl; **st**, stitch; **sl**, slip; **tog**, together; **dec**, decrease (by taking 2 sts tog); **inc**, increase (by working twice in same st); **up1**, pick up loop lying between needles and k into the back of it; **ss**, stocking st (k on right side and p on wrong side); **skpo**, sl1, k1, pass sl st over; **k1d**, k next st 1 row down.

NOTE

Yarn amounts are based on average requirements and are therefore approx. Figures in square brackets worked as stated after 2nd bracket.

Easy-peasy

A Bit More Tricky

Hard-ish

Quite A Challenge

HAT

Side: With 3¾mm needles and using two strands of yarn together, cast on 110 sts.
Beginning with a k row, ss 9 rows for hem facing.
K 1 row for foldline.
Change to 4mm needles.
Beginning with a k row, ss 50 rows. Cast off.
Top: With 3¾mm needles and using two strands of yarn together, cast on 8 sts. P 1 row.
Next row: Cast on 2, k to last st, inc kwise in last st.
Next row: Cast on 2, p to last st, inc pwise in last st.
Repeat last 2 rows, once more – 20 sts.
Continue in ss and inc 1 st at each end of next 3 rows and 5 following alternate rows – 36 sts.
Ss 13 rows.
Dec 1 st at each end of next row and 5 following alternate rows, then on next 2 rows – 20 sts.
Next row: Cast off 2, p to last 2 sts, p2tog.
Next row: Cast off 2, k to last 2 sts, k2tog.
Repeat last 2 rows, once more – 8 sts.
Cast off.
Bow: With 4mm needles and using two strands of yarn together, cast on 25 sts.
1st row: Sl1, k to end.
2nd row: Sl1, [k1d, p1] to end.
These 2 rows form pattern.
Continue in pattern until bow measures 16cm, ending with 1st row. Cast off in pattern.
Bow tie: With 4mm needles and using two strands of yarn together, cast on 13 sts.
Work in pattern as on bow until tie measures 10cm, ending with a 1st row.
Cast off in pattern.
To make up: Join row-ends of side together.
Fold hem facing at foldline to wrong side and slip stitch in position. Sew in top to cast-off edge of side with backstitch. Join row-ends of bow tie. With this seam at centre of underside, wrap tie round centre of bow and join ends of tie at back.
Sew bow to hat.

BAG

Back: With 3¾mm needles and using three strands of Red together, cast on 40 sts.
Beginning with a k row, ss 7 rows for top edge facing.
K 1 row for foldline.
Change to 4mm needles.
Beginning with a k row, ss 12 rows.
Increase row: K10, up1, k to last 10 sts, up1, k10. Ss 11 rows.
Repeat last 12 rows, twice more then work increase row again – 48 sts.
Ss 3 rows.
Base: Mark each end of last row.
Ss 42 rows. Mark each end of last row.
Front: Ss another 2 rows.
Dec row: K10, skpo, k to last 12 sts, k2tog, k10. Ss 11 rows.
Repeat last 12 rows, twice more, then work dec row again – 40 sts.
Ss 12 rows.
Change to 3¾mm needles.
K 1 row for foldline.
Beginning with a k row, ss 7 rows for top edge facing.
Cast off pwise.
Gusset: With 3¾mm needles and using three strands of Red together, cast on 16 sts.
Beginning with a k row, ss 7 rows for top edge facing.
K 1 row for foldline.
Change to 4mm needles.
Beginning with a k row, ss 12 rows.
Increase row: K5, up1, k to last 5 sts, up1, k5. Ss 5 rows.
Repeat last 6 rows, 5 times more, then work increase row again – 30 sts.
Ss 3 rows.
Mark each end of last row.
Ss 68 rows for base lining.
Mark each end of last row.
Ss another 2 rows.
Dec row: K5, skpo, k to last 7 sts, k2tog, k5. Ss 5 rows.
Repeat last 6 rows, 5 times more, then work dec row again – 16 sts.
Ss 12 rows.
Change to 3¾mm needles.
K 1 row for foldline.
Beginning with a k row, ss 7 rows for top edge facing. Cast off pwise.
Tab: With 4mm needles and using three strands of Red together, cast on 30 sts.
Beginning with a k row, ss 9 rows.

K 1 row for foldline.
Beginning with a k row, ss 8 rows.
Opening for fastening row:
K10, cast off next 10 sts, k to end.
Next row: P10, cast on 10 sts, p to end. Ss 8 rows.
P 1 row for foldline.
Beginning with a p row, ss 9 rows. Cast off.
Handle: With 4mm needles and using three strands of Red together, cast on 66 sts.
Beginning with a k row, ss 5 rows.
K 1 row for foldline.
Beginning with a k row, ss 10 rows.
P 1 row for foldline.
Beginning with a p row, ss 5 rows. Cast off.
Bow: With 4mm needles and using three strands of Grey together, cast on 25 sts.
1st row: Sl1, k to end.
2nd row: Sl1, [k1d, p1] to end.
These 2 rows form pattern.
Continue in pattern until bow measures 16cm, ending with a 1st row. Cast off in pattern.
Bow tie: With 4mm needles and using three strands of Grey together, cast on 13 sts.
Work in pattern as on bow until tie measures 10cm, ending with a 1st row. Cast off in pattern.
To back: Pin gusset to main piece, matching markers and taking gusset base along inside of bag base. Join the four side seams, then working on the inside, slip stitch gusset base in position. Slip stitch bag base to gusset on the outside along one side. Insert stiffener or stout card into base and slip stitch remaining side. Fold hem at foldline to wrong side and slip stitch in position. Fold sides of tab at foldlines, and join cast-on and cast-off edges together, leaving opening to match top layer. Join short ends together and neaten edges around slit. Sew one end of tab inside top edge at centre of back. Fold handle at foldlines and join seam at centre for underside. Join short ends together and sew to bag. Join row-ends of bow tie. With this seam at centre of underside, wrap tie round centre of bow and join ends of tie at back. Sew bow to front of bag level with tab slit.

POST – CARD

Reader Carole Killiner, from Preston in Lancashire, nominates the Austrian Tyrol

'The Austrian Tyrol must be one of the most beautiful places in the world. My husband and I have visited several of the resorts over the last 20 years. The majestic mountains and gentle, rolling meadows are all easily accessible by the efficiently run cable-car system. The view from one of the higher paths overlooking Neustift is a particular favourite of mine.'

2 Monday

3 Tuesday

4 Wednesday

5 Thursday

6 Friday

7 Saturday

8 Sunday

Handmade
Cards To Treasure

Use scraps of paper to create these simple and attractive festive designs

Collaged Christmas Tree

Craft tip
If you use wrapping paper with text on it, you can cut out one of the festive messages to use on your Christmas card.

Typography

COLLAGED CHRISTMAS TREE

- 13 x 18cm brown card blank
- A selection of different patterned papers
- Pencil
- Scissors
- Glue

1 Enlarge the tree template (below right) by 200% on a photocopier and cut out. Using our photograph as a guide, use a pencil to draw scallops on to the tree shape – each section you draw will be a different piece of paper.

2 Cut out the sections of the tree, then use them as templates to draw round on the back of your chosen papers. Cut out the shapes.

3 Arrange the papers in order on the front of your card. Once you are satisfied, stick them all in place starting from the trunk and working your way up.

4 Either write or stamp your festive message on to white paper and stick it to a piece of coloured paper to frame it. Finally, glue it just below the trunk of the tree.

TYPOGRAPHY

- 10cm square white card blank
- 3 different patterned papers
- Green paper
- Pencil
- Scissors
- Glue

1 Enlarge the typography templates (below right) by 200% on a photocopier and use them to cut out the festive words from three different patterned papers.

2 Arrange on the card front, using our photograph as a guide. Once you are happy with the arrangement, glue in place.

3 Cut two stars from green paper and glue either side of the word 'Joy'.

MINI STAR

- 5.5 x 6.5cm white card blank (or cut one to size)
- 2 patterned papers
- Button
- Scissors
- Glue

1 Enlarge the star templates (right) by 400%, twice, on a photocoper. Cut away outer frame from one, then use to cut stars from two different patterned papers.

2 Stick the small star to the large star, then glue to centre of the card.

3 To finish, glue a button to the centre of the star.

Mini Star

Button Tree

BUTTON TREE

- 15 x 10cm white card blank
- 14 round buttons
- 1 star button (optional)
- Papers in brown, pink and green
- Tracing paper and a pencil
- Scissors
- Glue

1 Cut a 7 x 0.5cm strip of brown paper for the trunk. Then either draw 10 curly branches, or cut them out freehand from brown paper, varying the lengths and the widths.

2 Cut out a 3 x 2cm pot from pink paper, cutting it slightly narrower towards the bottom. Trace off the star template (right) and cut from green paper.

3 Arrange all the paper pieces on the card front. Once you are happy with the arrangement, stick them all in place.

4 Finally, stick buttons to the branches and a star button within the paper star at the top of the tree.

TEMPLATES

Enlarge on a photocopier or trace on to paper at actual size, according to individual card instructions

HO JOY twinkle

Feature and styling: Emily Dawe. Photos: Stewart Grant. Illustrations: Terry Evans. Papers from a selection at Paperchase (paperchase.co.uk) and Caroline Gardner (carolinegardner.com). Buttons, John Lewis (johnlewis.com). Card blanks and mini buttons, Hobbycraft (hobbycraft.co.uk)

Your Good Health

Ask Dr Mel

Q Health-monitoring apps seem to be very popular at the moment, and there's a huge selection to choose from. Are they a good idea?

A There are now thousands of these mobile phone/tablet applications devoted to health-related issues. For example, you can monitor and record things such as your weight, exercise, sleep, mood, blood pressure, calorie/alcohol intake, and so on, download almost any type of diet or fitness program, or even learn to meditate or brush your teeth properly. Other apps provide details about specific diseases, and help you keep track of your own condition and medication, or provide information for your doctor (but keep it simple, please!). You can also set goals, and inform friends on social media of your progress, and update your device wherever you go.

However, some of these apps do need a health warning. For example, like many internet websites, they're not all designed by experts and so may contain inaccurate, biased or just plain wacky information. Vulnerable users may feel pressured into setting inappropriate goals. And, as many apps 'harvest' your data, there is some concern about where it could end up, who might use it (insurers? employers?) and how.

But taking responsibility for your own health is always a good idea, so long as you choose your apps carefully.

TAKE 4...
Ways To Cut Breast Cancer Risk

1 MAINTAIN a healthy weight after the menopause – fat cells raise oestrogen levels.

2 A HEALTHY DIET (less saturated fat, more fibre, calcium and a rainbow of fruit and veg) may help.

3 KEEP ACTIVE – 30 minutes' exercise five times a week could cut your risk by a fifth.

4 STICK to recommended alcohol limits – no more than 14-21 units a week (small glass of wine = 1.5 units).

A Great Exercise To...
Stretch the hips, hamstrings and glutes

Knee hugs

Stand with your feet shoulder-width apart and your arms at your sides. Step forward with your left leg, bend your knee. Lift your right foot off the ground, grasp it with both hands just below the kneecap and pull it as close to your chest as you can. Release the leg. Repeat on the other side. Keep alternating until you've done five times on each side.
Well done!

TIP
Make it more dynamic by taking three steps forward between each time.

HOW THE EXPERTS STAY HEALTHY

Danielle Collins, yoga teacher, well-being coach, relaxation therapist and face-yoga expert

What do you always keep in your medicine cabinet?
Aloe vera and coconut oil, for dry skin, sunburn and rashes (I mix equal amounts of the two together for a fab body moisturiser). And Olbas Oil, to relieve a blocked nose.

What's good in your fridge?
Carrots, apples and fresh ginger to juice, for essential nutrients – this boosts my energy levels and is a great way to get lots of goodness in one glass. I always have lemons; I drink the juice in hot water and squeeze on to salads and fish as a healthy way to add flavour.

What's your favourite health routine?
Yoga – it's great for building strength and flexibility, as well as calming and energising the mind. My face-yoga method works out all the muscles of the face and it helps to smooth, tighten and freshen my skin.

Any childhood remedies you still use?
My mum always had a cup of camomile tea before bed. I've carried on that routine and I find it's a great way to feel calm and sleepy.
● Visit faceyogaexpert.com

9 Monday

10 Tuesday

11 Wednesday

12 Thursday

13 Friday

14 Saturday

15 Sunday

Bacon & Sweetcorn Potatoes

Serves 6-12
Calories: 210
Fat: 9g
Saturated fat: 3.5g
Suitable for freezing: ✗

* 6 baking potatoes
* 12 rashers smoked streaky bacon, chopped
* 1tbsp light olive oil
* 4tbsp crème fraîche
* 198g can sweetcorn, drained
* 1 bunch spring onions, sliced
* Chopped fresh parsley, for garnish

1 Set the oven to 200°C or Gas Mark 6. Wash the potatoes and prick the skins, then bake them for 1-1¼ hours, or until they feel tender when pressed. Remove from the oven and keep them warm.

2 Cook the bacon in the oil in a frying pan until crispy. Remove it from the pan and drain on absorbent kitchen paper.

3 Cut the potatoes in half and scoop the centres into a bowl, then place the skin shells on a baking tray. Add the crème fraîche to the potato and mash until smooth. Stir in the bacon, sweetcorn and spring onion, and season. Spoon the mixture back into the potato skins.

4 Return the potatoes to the oven and cook for about 15 minutes, or until the filling is just starting to turn golden. Remove from the oven and scatter over chopped parsley, then serve immediately.

Learning To Leap

The world was opening up to Kathy in more ways than one, but was she running when she should be walking, taking it one step at a time?

Kathy leaned back on her elbows. The sun was climbing higher in the sky, warming her skin. It was so easy, laying there, doing nothing, something she was just getting used to. It had never been like this with Keith. She'd been awkward then, constantly adjusting her bikini straps, making sure she was behaving appropriately as he liked to put it. That's what she could never understand, that double-edged sword that constantly dangled over her head. He was proud of her, wanted to show her off, encouraging her to wear the skimpiest of bikinis that she never felt comfortable in. He wanted other men to look...and when they did...well, then it was her fault, wasn't it? She wanted to leave him didn't she? She was doing it all to spite him?

She hadn't of course, wanted to leave him, not in the beginning. She thought it was love, this constant, devoted attention – before it turned into something darker. The memory made her shudder despite the heat and she wrapped her arms about herself. Mike sat up beside her.

'Cold?' his voice was edged with concern.

She shook her head, used her hand to shield her eyes to look at him.

'No, I'm fine. An involuntary shiver.'

'Let me warm you up then.' He kissed her and she closed her eyes and felt the sun beat down upon them both.

He drew back, leaving her breathless and the pair of them sat side by side watching a group of teenagers jump off nearby rocks, squealing with delight as they splashed into the waters below. With endless energy they would swim back to the shore, scramble up the rocks and wait their turn to do it again.

'Looks fun,' said Mike.

'Looks like punishment,' Kathy replied. 'It's like skiing – fine going down but boring going back to the top again.'

'Ah, but that's all part of it, can't have the fun without effort.'

They watched as a young girl hesitated for a moment, looking down at the water, her friends urging her forwards with smiles and encouragement. After much persuasion the girl leapt out, eyes closed, face scrunched up with tension and emerged moments later, a huge smile on her face as she swam back to shore.

Kathy recognised that hesitance, that feeling of being afraid to leap, wondering if you would, in fact, emerge with a smile. Keith had shrunken her world bit by bit. She had mistaken his caring and protectiveness for kindness and security. It didn't take long to discover it was anything but. It had knocked her confidence, left her afraid to step out into the world for a long time. But she had stepped out. In the end. And now here she was in southern Spain, another step forward. The world was opening up to her in more ways than one but she wondered now if she was ready for it. Was she running when she should be walking, taking it one step at a time?

She knew Mike was going to propose tonight. She could tell by his body language. She knew how to spot the signs, she was an expert thanks to Keith; that indiscernible shift in movement, in attitude, visible only to her. But a ring? She wasn't sure. Was she ready for that commitment again? What if it went wrong a second time? Would she be able to recover?

The young people by the rocks began to drift away.

'I fancy a bit of fun now the coast's clear,' Mike said, standing up and casting a shadow over her. 'Coming?'

She shook her head. 'Not yet.' She wasn't ready. 'I'll watch.'

She stood beside him as he prepared to dive. His body was still lean and taut and she watched him jump into the crystal blue waters below. He disappeared before resurfacing and shaking the water from his hair. His face was a golden brown now, and a brilliant smile broke on his face as he brushed his hair back with his hands.

'Come on in,' he called from the water, beckoning her with the sweep of his arm, 'you'll love it.'

Mike scrambled back up the rocks and held out his hand, clasping hers. He was gentle and it was not the hold of a brute, not the possessive, tight grip that told her there would be consequences when they got home if she didn't do as she was told. Not the grip that pinched her fingers and crushed them against her rings into her flesh. Holding her back not holding her up. There was real strength in Mike's hand, but there was softness too; a cushion.

'It's so refreshing,' he said. 'Jump with me?'

'I'm afraid,' she said quietly. She could admit that to him, knowing he wouldn't take advantage, wouldn't force her to do anything she didn't want to. And as the realisation settled upon her she felt lighter and knew that she would float, would resurface. This was different.

She gazed down on the water, sunlight reflecting on the ripples, dappled by shade from the trees above now that the sun had moved. The air was heavy with the smell of eucalyptus and wild rosemary that grew in the woodland around the lakes.

She could do this.

'Take all the time you need,' he said. 'We'll do it together.'

He stood beside her, strong and silent, waiting until she had built up her courage, waiting until she was sure.

'Ready?' he asked.

She smiled back at him. Yes, she was ready and when he asked, as she knew he would, she knew what her answer would be. There was nothing to think about, nothing to consider. She just had to jump.

And she did.

THE END

© Francine Lee, 2013

> *And now here she was in southern Spain*

16 Monday

17 Tuesday

18 Wednesday

19 Thursday

20 Friday

21 Saturday

22 Sunday

Number fit

All you have to do is fit these numbers into the grid, reading across and down.

3 DIGITS
150
308
726
758
784
791
931
957
988

4 DIGITS
3120
7780
9501

5 DIGITS
10442
11612
90219

6 DIGITS
118407
271184
787663

7 DIGITS
1827676
2242874
4765814

8 DIGITS
23654051
34225500
87020181

9 DIGITS
398260263
622710681
965689456

Sudoku 2

To solve this puzzle, fill in the grid so that each 3 x 3 box, each row and each column contains the numbers 1-9.

You can work it out...

		9	4		5		3	
			1					
6					7			4
7	4					5		9
					2			
1		2		9			6	8
			7					6
2					9			5
		5	2		6	1	8	

Solutions to this month's puzzles on December puzzles

SOLUTIONS FOR SEPTEMBER 2015

Answer: SCONE

23 Monday

24 Tuesday

25 Wednesday

26 Thursday

27 Friday

28 Saturday

29 Sunday

DECEMBER

30 Monday

1 Tuesday

2 Wednesday

3 Thursday

4 Friday

5 Saturday

6 Sunday

Bakewell Mince Pies

Makes 21-24
Calories: 196
Fat: 11g
Saturated fat: 4.5g
Suitable for freezing: ✔

FOR THE PASTRY:
* 100g (3½oz) chilled butter, cut into slivers
* 175g (6oz) plain flour
* Pinch of salt
* 1 tablespoon caster sugar
* 1 large egg yolk

FOR THE TOPPING:
* 90g (3oz) butter, softened
* 90g (3oz) caster sugar
* 90g (3oz) ground almonds
* 30g (1oz) plain flour
* 1 large egg, beaten
* 1 tablespoon amaretto, rum, brandy or Calvados
* 410g jar good mincemeat with a grated apple or 30g (1oz) more dried fruit added
* A few flaked almonds, optional
* Icing sugar, for dusting

* 8cm (3¼in) plain cutter
* 2 trays of 12-hole patty tins

1 To make the pastry: Rub the butter into the flour, salt and sugar until the mixture looks like breadcrumbs. Stir in the egg yolk with 1 tablespoon cold water and work with a knife until it binds together. Or, use a food processor. Knead a little, shape into a flat square, then wrap it in a polybag and chill for about 15 minutes.

2 To make the topping: Beat the butter until soft, beat in the sugar, then the ground almonds, flour, egg and alcohol. Cover and chill while you roll out the pastry.

3 Cut the pastry block in half. Roll out one piece as thinly as you can (3mm/⅛in) and cut out rounds to line the patty tins. Roll out the other piece, cut out more rounds, and then collect all the trimmings up, roll out and cut more rounds. Mark the edges lightly with a fork. Chill them while the oven heats up to 180°C or Gas Mark 4.

4 Spoon just under a tablespoon of mincemeat into each case, then top with 2 teaspoons of almond topping to use it all up. Sprinkle with flaked almonds, if you like. Bake for 35 minutes until golden, switching the trays around in the oven halfway through. Cool for 5 minutes, then take out of the tins carefully (as the pastry is thin) and cool on a wire rack.
   Dust with icing sugar for serving. Sprinkle it over a star-shaped stencil, if you like.

POST – CARD

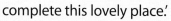

Reader Dorothy Organ, from Epping, nominates Trevone in North Cornwall

'This is a seaside resort with a split personality. Follow the lane down the hill and just as you see the sea, it splits. Turn right for a beautiful sheltered sandy bay – perfect for beach games, sandcastles and just lolling about. Turn left for a rocky seashore with warm pools – ideal for paddling or searching for crabs. A store and café beside the beach complete this lovely place.'

7 Monday

8 Tuesday

9 Wednesday

10 Thursday

11 Friday

12 Saturday

13 Sunday

Toasty Toes

Cosy knitted slippers with a fluffy warm lining – a winter essential!

MEASUREMENTS
To fit foot: Child size 28/29 and adult size 38/39.

MATERIALS
1 (2) x 50g (50m) ball(s) of Rico Design Creative Filz in Jeans (28) or Grey (91); 1 x 50g (80m) ball of Rico Design Fashion Fur in Cream (01). Pair of 8mm (No. 0) and 4½mm (No. 7) knitting needles; a cable needle; a pair of Rico leather slipper soles in size 28/29 for a child and 38/39 for an adult. You can buy the yarn and leather slipper soles from womansweeklyshop.com

TENSION
11 stitches and 17 rows, to 10 x 10cm, over stocking stitch, using 8mm needles and Creative Filz, and 13 stitches and 25 rows, to 10 x 10cm, over garter stitch, using 4½mm needles and Fashion Fur.

ABBREVIATIONS
K, knit; **p**, purl; **st**, stitch; **gst**, garter stitch; **inc**, increase (by working twice into same st); **sl**, slip; **dec**, decrease (by working 2 sts together); **gst**, garter stitch (every row k); **cr3lt**, cross 3 left (sl next 2 sts on to cable needle and leave at front, p1, k2 from cable needle); **cr4lt**, cross 4 left (sl next 3 sts on to cable needle and leave at front, p1, k3 from cable needle); **cr3rt**, cross 3 right (sl next st on to cable needle and leave at back, k2, p1 from cable needle); **cr4rt**, cross 4 right (sl next st on to cable needle and leave at back, k3, p1 from cable needle); **c4f**, cable 4 front (sl next 2 sts on to cable needle and leave at front, k2, then k2 from cable needle); **c6f**, cable 6 front (sl next 3 sts on to cable needle and leave at front, k3, then k3 from cable needle); **up1**, pick up loop lying between needles and k into back of it.

NOTE
Yarn amounts are based on average requirements and are approximate. Instructions in square brackets are worked as stated after 2nd bracket.

row-ends from first inc row to cast-on edge.
1st row (wrong side): K2, p2, k1. **2nd row:** P1, k2, p2. **3rd to 13th rows:** Repeat last 2 rows, 5 times, then work 1st row. Mark end of last row. **14th row:** P1, k2, up1, p2 – 6 sts. **15th row:** K2, p3, k1. **16th row:** P1, k3, p2. **17th row:** As 15th row. **18th row:** P1, k3, up1, p2 – 7 sts. **19th row:** K2, p4, k1. **20th row:** P1, k4, p2. **21st row:** As 19th row. **22nd row:** P1, k4, up1, p2 – 8 sts. **23rd row:** K2, p5, k1. **24th row:** P1, k5, p2. **25th row:** As 23rd row.
With wrong side of sides facing, having right sides together and needles pointing in the same direction, cast off, taking 1 st from each needle and k them together.

LININGS (make 2)
Sole: With 4½mm needles and Cream, cast on 4 sts. Gst 2 rows. Continue in gst and inc 1 st at each end of next row and following alternate row – 8 sts. Gst 17 rows. ** Mark each end of last row. Gst another 18 rows. Dec 1 st at each end of next row and following alternate row – 4 sts. Gst 1 row. Cast off.
Top: Work as sole to **. Cast off.
Sides: With 4mm needles and Cream, cast on 45 sts loosely. Gst 4 rows. **Next row:** Cast off 12 sts, k to last 12 sts, cast off these 12 sts, turn and rejoin yarn to remaining 21 sts. Continuing in gst, cast off 2 sts at beginning of next 6 rows – 9 sts. Cast off.

CHILD'S SLIPPERS
UPPERS (make 2)
With 8mm needles and Jeans, cast on 8 sts.
1st row (right side): P1, k2, p2, k2, p1. **2nd row:** K1, p2, k2, p2, k1. **3rd and 4th rows:** Repeat 1st and 2nd rows, once. **5th row:** Inc, cr3lt, cr3rt, inc – 10 sts. **6th row:** K3, p4, k3. **7th row:** P3, c4f, p3. **8th row:** As 6th row. **9th row:** P2, cr3rt, cr3lt, p2. **10th row:** K2, [p2, k2] twice. **11th row:** P2, [k2, p2] twice. **12th to 14th rows:** Work 10th and 11th rows, once, then work 10th row. **15th row:** P2, cr3lt, cr3rt, p2. **16th to 18th rows:** Work 6th and 7th rows, once, then work 6th row. Cast off firmly.
First side: With right side facing, using 8mm needles and Jeans, pick up and k5 sts along row-ends from cast-on edge to first inc row.
1st row (wrong side): K1, p2, k2. **2nd row:** P2, k2, p1. **3rd to 13th rows:** Repeat last 2 rows, 5 times more, then work 1st row. Mark beginning of last row. **14th row:** P2, up1, k2, p1 – 6 sts. **15th row:** K1, p3, k2. **16th row:** P2, k3, p1. **17th row:** As 15th row. **18th row:** P2, up1, k3, p1 – 7 sts. **19th row:** K1, p4, k2. **20th row:** P2, k4, p1. **21st row:** As 19th row. **22nd row:** P2, up1, k4, p1 – 8 sts. **23rd row:** K1, p5, k2. **24th row:** P2, k5, p1. **25th row:** As 23rd row. Leave these sts on a safety pin.
Second side: With right side facing, using 8mm needles and Jeans, pick up and k5 sts along opposite

ADULT'S SLIPPERS
UPPERS (make 2)
With 8mm needles and Grey, cast on 12 sts. **1st row (right side):** P2, [k3, p2] twice. **2nd row:** K2, [p3, k2] twice. **3rd to 6th rows:** Repeat 1st and 2nd rows, twice. **7th row:** Inc, p1, cr4lt, cr4rt, p1, inc – 14 sts. **8th row:** Inc,

k3, p6, k3, inc – 16 sts. **9th row:** P5, c6f, p5. **10th row:** K5, p6, k5. **11th row:** P4, cr4rt, cr4lt, p4. **12th row:** K4, p3, k2, p3, k4. **13th row:** P4, k3, p2, k3, p4. **14th to 18th rows:** Repeat 12th and 13th rows, twice, then work 12th row. **19th row:** P4, cr4lt, cr4rt, p4. **20th row:** As 10th row. **21st and 22nd rows:** As 9th and 10th rows. **23rd row:** P5, k6 p5. **24th row:** As 10th row. Cast off firmly.

First side: With right side facing, using 8mm needles and Grey, pick up and k6 sts along row-ends from cast-on edge to first inc row. **1st row:** K1, p3, k2. **2nd row:** P2, k3, p1. **3rd to 19th rows:** Repeat last 2 rows, 8 times more, then work 1st row. Mark beginning of last row. **20th row:** P2, up1, k3, p1 – 7 sts. **21st row:** K1, p4, k2. **22nd row:** P2, k4, p1. **23rd row:** As 21st row. **24th row:** P2, up1, k4, p1 – 8 sts. **25th row:** K1, p5, k2. **26th row:** P2, k5, p1. **27th row:** As 25th row. Continue as before and inc 1 st on next row and 2 following 4th rows – 11 sts. Work 3 rows

straight. Leave sts on a st holder.
Second side: With right side facing, using 8mm needles and Grey, pick up and k6 sts along opposite row-ends from first inc row to cast-on edge. **1st row:** K2, p3, k1. **2nd row:** P1, k3, p2. **3rd to 19th rows:** Repeat last 2 rows, 8 times more, then work 1st row. Mark end of last row. **20th row:** P1, k3, up1, p2 – 7 sts. **21st row:** K2, p4, k1. **22nd row:** P1, k4, p2. **23rd row:** As 21st row. **24th row:** P1, k4, up1, p2 – 8 sts. **25th row:** K2, p5, k1. **26th row:** P1, k5, p2. **27th row:** As 25th row. Continue as before and inc 1 st on next row and 2 following 4th rows – 11 sts. Work 3 rows straight. With wrong side of sides facing, having right sides together and needles pointing in the same direction, cast off, taking 1 st from each needle and k them together.

LININGS (make 2)

Sole: With 4½mm needles and Cream, cast on 8 sts. Gst 2 rows. Continue in gst and inc 1 st at each

end of next row and following alternate row – 12 sts. Gst 27 rows. ** Mark each end of last row. Gst another 28 rows. Dec 1 st at each end of next row and following alternate row – 8 sts. Gst 1 row. Cast off.
Top: Work as sole to **. Cast off.
Sides: With 4mm and Cream, cast on 63 sts loosely. Gst 6 rows. **Next row:** Cast off 16 sts, k to last 16 sts, cast off these 16 sts, turn and rejoin yarn to remaining 31 sts. Continuing in gst, cast off 2 sts at beginning of next 8 rows – 15 sts. Cast off.

TO MAKE UP

For centre front seam, join short row-ends of sides lining together. Sew cast-off edges of sides to outer edge of soles. Sew tops to sides, ending level with markers on soles. Sew row-ends of uppers to row-ends of sides as far as markers. Insert lining into uppers; tack in position to edge of soles. Stitch tops to linings around open top edges. With matching yarn, blanket-stitch slippers to leather soles.

Designer: Shirley Bradford

The Jazz Age

Some women got to dance wildly all through the night. But most had a tamer time, albeit an increasingly glamorous one

Feline Felix The world-famous cat first appeared in a comic strip in 1923 and went on to become a silent cartoon star

The lure of fame For the first time, many women of all classes and ages aspired to be famous – primarily by becoming a star of the screen. Hollywood was to blame with the allure of the extravagance, glamour, hedonism, and fun displayed in the movies. Actresses were seen as strong and a little enigmatic – and fabulously rich!

14 Monday

15 Tuesday

16 Wednesday

17 Thursday

18 Friday

19 Saturday

20 Sunday

THE Guardian

Forty-five years we've watched him. He likes to rearrange the decorations, no matter how humble the tree. I respect a guy who takes pride in how we look, and doesn't take us for granted...

There's this legend, perhaps you've come across it, that at midnight on Christmas Eve all the animals can talk or some such. An old story about the beasts in Bethlehem got it started. Now I don't want to be the one to burst your bubble, but quite frankly, that ain't the half of it. For a start, the timing thing is a bit woolly. Events, you might say, were a tad distracting. Face it: there wasn't a stopwatch in the stable. Stuff happened, keeps happening every year, and it's not just the animals.

From my vantage point on the top of the tree I get to see a fair bit of comings and goings. Just because I have flyaway blonde hair and a flouncy white outfit doesn't make me some sort of Sleeping Beauty. At least they got the wings about right. I mean, if you bumped into Gabriel or Raphael you wouldn't dare accuse them of being 'cute' or 'pretty'. 'Awesome' is more like it.

Anyway, come Christmas Eve I get to see it all, and chat to the regulars on my team. The doves never stop billing and cooing over the decorations and the slipping standards of present wrapping. The robin is far more optimistic, convinced Spring, sunshine and all things wonderful are just another dawn away. He's effortlessly upbeat, which can be a bit tiring. Tin soldier's pretty tight-lipped. Some guys just never seem to unwind. Looks a bit lost, if you ask me – no comrades, no mess room to frolic in. Just hanging around. Mind you, I reckon he's got his eye on that ballet dancer they always perch up near me. She's a sweet thing, but her stares are a bit full-on, like she's dreaming of getting up close and personal. A guy can't help it if he oozes charisma. But she hasn't got a hope – not in my job description, see. She really ought to give Private Meek a chance. They'd be good together.

Tree's not so big this year. We're crammed on a four-footer up on a tabletop. Lot of my mates got left in the box, no room on the branches. Still, smells like the crowd is going to come round to keep the old folks company. She's got the ham roasting and it smells grand. 'Saves room for the turkey tomorrow,' she always tells him, though he hardly listens. It'll all be fine, no matter how she fusses. It always is. He's placed his parcels for Private Meek to guard. Forty-five years we've

> She's got the ham roasting and it smells grand. 'Saves room for the turkey tomorrow'

watched him. A roll of paper and some sticky tape always at the last minute; a chore to him, not an art form. The art comes in taking time to choose the right gift. He finds it hard to resist rearranging those garlands. The symmetry matters, no matter how humble the tree. I respect a guy who takes pride in how we look. Doesn't take us for granted.

He has grandkids asleep upstairs. They took ages to settle. Santa DVDs, hot baths, stories, warm milk, the lot. Just before their round of goodnight kisses, they came into view. Very gingerly carrying a plate of mince pies, a pint glass and a bottle of Guinness. A must-have snack for Father Christmas by the hearth. They left their named sacks beside the nightcap, just so the old fella wouldn't forget.

As silence finally fell on the gigglers, Grandad returned. I had to smile. He was carrying a pair of wellington boots, and a mesh strainer. Grandma followed, handing him the icing sugar. Gently shaking the sugar around the boots, Santa's snowy footprints emerged from the chimney. The young ones will be astonished, convinced by absolute proof. The older ones might have their doubts about snowflakes that don't seem to melt, but I'm betting they'll let it pass.

With a burst of icy air embracing them, the young parents returned. Pubs were heaving with revellers, they said, rather too loudly. Certainly merry. They tiptoed upstairs to bring down their offerings. 'Better wrapped, quality paper,' cooed the doves.

'John Lewis or Next?' queried the ballerina.

The soft glow of the fairy lights fell on their faces as I watched them. They're a solid couple, these two. They'll go the distance. Maybe I'll get passed on to their tree one day, if someone can sort out my hair.

They sit together on the couch, talking softly, only the tree lights on. In charge while the oldies escape to midnight Mass. Too snuggled up to hear our whisperings. I reckon it's a good year. No telling what I'll catch sight of next year, but my instincts tell me they can cope. Arm in arm, they, too, head off to bed.

Pretty soon the old couple will get back. I'll watch her check the timings for the morning's cooking; he'll slip in and unplug the lights. When I reawaken, close to midnight next year, I hope they'll both still be here, a little more lined, more grey, but still letting me watch over them.

THE END

© Kate Myers, 2013

21 Monday

22 Tuesday

23 Wednesday

24 Thursday

25 Friday CHRISTMAS DAY

26 Saturday BOXING DAY

27 Sunday

Have A Go At...

Festive Flower Decorations

Put together these magical Christmas table and chair
arrangements in 30 minutes or less

You will need

- **A 20cm-wide square watertight container or vase**
- **A block of Oasis foam big enough to fit inside your square container**
- **1 pack each of Sparkle Foliage (eucalyptus, gypsophila and eryngium);**
- **1 pack of white short-stemmed Sweetheart Sparkle Roses;**
- **1 short, wide white candle, find similar from a selection at M&S**
- **Sharp scissors**
- **Bread knife**
- **3 x garden canes**
- **Sellotape**

1 Take the block of Oasis and place it in a bowl of cold water until it is totally immersed. Avoid pushing it under the water as this creates air bubbles that can affect the flower stems. Using a bread knife, cut the Oasis to fit your vase, ensuring the top is just proud of the rim.

2 Tape the canes in place evenly around the candle. Using scissors, cut across each stick, leaving about 2in. Push in the centre of the Oasis.

3 Taking the frosted eucalyptus, cut stems to required length, removing any leaves from the bottom 2in. Place around the base of candle at about 45-degree angles, leaving plenty of gaps. Your foliage can be slightly different heights – there's no need to be too rigid about it all being exactly the same size.

4 Cut the gypsophila to your required length, again leaving the bottom 2in clean of any leaves. Use it to fill in any gaps. Now do the same with the eryngium.

5 Take your pack of white roses, trim down the stems and dot them in your arrangement for the final touch. Add more of the foliage to fill in any gaps, if required.

Our tip

Odd numbers look good, so we used three groups of three roses around the candle.

Sitting Pretty

TO MAKE THE CHAIR DECORATION:
Take 3 stems of eucalyptus, 1 stem of cotton and 1 stem of berries, secure with ribbon and attach to chair.
Cotton and Ilex Berry Bouquet; eucalyptus from Sparkle Foliage, find similar from a selection at M&S

CRYPTIC CROSSWORD

Fill in the crossword and rearrange the letters in the shaded squares to form the answer.

Clue: Sleeping but not behind the door (5).

ACROSS

1 When next inside home of the Acropolis (6)
5 Chaperone adjusting corset (6)
8 Lighted torch for Father Brown's assistant (8)
9 Cut of meat and drink, introduction to picnic (4)
10 Soap suds regularly work (4)
11 Taking advantage is grand (8)
12 Stick with business in this place (6)
13 Fool given first aid (6)
15 In partnership it's needed to secure the woman (8)
18 Race around tree (4)
19 A one-off time period (4)
20 I leave religious service to get military weapons (8)
21 Effects as groups (6)
22 Extremely clever soprano's part (4,2)

DOWN

2 The one to spell out camera accessory (9,4)
3 Seamen travelling round Spithead all together (2,5)
4 Litres spilt, with lemonade finally lacking vitality (7)
5 Provide witticism after end of tale (5)
6 Kings and queens, perhaps, eccentric types (5)
7 Crime scenes in rambling anecdotes (13)
13 Shorten a spanner? (7)
14 Bird a very long time in southern seaside town (7)
16 Wise Premium Bond selector (5)
17 Shook off boxers' blows (5)

You can work it out...

Solutions to this month's puzzle on January puzzles

SOLUTIONS FOR NOVEMBER 2015

8	7	9	4	2	5	6	3	1
5	3	4	1	6	8	9	7	2
6	2	1	9	3	7	8	5	4
7	4	3	6	8	1	5	2	9
9	8	6	5	7	2	4	1	3
1	5	2	3	9	4	7	6	8
4	1	8	7	5	3	2	9	6
2	6	7	8	1	9	3	4	5
3	9	5	2	4	6	1	8	7

28 Monday BANK HOLIDAY

29 Tuesday

30 Wednesday

31 Thursday

1 Jan 2016 NEW YEAR'S DAY

2 Jan 2016

3 Jan 2016